Rules for Retrogrades

Rules for Retrogrades

Forty Tactics to Defeat the Radical Left

Timothy J. Gordon
David R. Gordon

TAN Books
Gastonia, North Carolina

Cover design by Caroline Green

Cover image: Crusader Knight Helm, by draco77vector / Shutterstock

Library of Congress Control Number: 2019955092

ISBN: 978-1-5051-1593-2

Published in the United States by
TAN Books
PO Box 269
Gastonia, NC 28053
www.TANBooks.com

Printed in the United States of America

Contents

Foreword

We have never been more miserable. Despite historic peace and material prosperity, surveys show happiness has declined steadily in the United States over the past half-century. A loneliness epidemic has overshadowed not just the United States but the entire Western world, and the problem only stands to get worse, as young people report feeling lonely more often and more intensely than any other age group. Marriage rates have plummeted, as have birth rates, which have now fallen below replacement. Each year abortion claims the lives of a million babies in the United States alone. We can no longer even agree on the definitions of "man" and "woman."

Saul Alinsky must be looking up from the afterlife with pride. Alinsky's *Rules For Radicals* inspired some of the most prominent progressive politicians in recent history, including former president Barack Obama and former secretary of state Hillary Clinton, with whom the author of those rules exchanged gushing letters. The progressive training manual worked, and the results have been hell—fitting, since Alinsky dedicated his book in part to Lucifer, "the first radical known to man who rebelled against the establishment and did it so effectively that he at least won his own kingdom."

Can "progress" breed misery? Chesterton considered progress a "useless word, for progress takes for granted an already defined direction: and it is exactly about the direction that we disagree." C. S. Lewis similarly observed, "We all want progress, but if you're on the wrong road, progress means doing an about-turn and walking back to the right road; in that case, the man who turns back soonest is the most progressive." Our civilization is dying: spiritually, culturally, and physically of old age. Each year the problem worsens. The only way forward is back.

In the inaugural issue of *National Review*, William F. Buckley Jr. defined the conservative's mission as standing "athwart history, yelling Stop, at a time when no one is inclined to do so." Timothy and David Gordon have more ambitious plans. A conservative might stop at standing, but the retrograde must go further. He cannot content himself with halting the inevitable march of a misery-making "progress." The retrograde takes a step back, not to relive some dead moment, but to recover something that has been lost.

One man's progressive is another man's retrograde. But the categories, whatever you like to call them, are not merely two sides of the same coin. Revering our cultural inheritance requires humility, the beginning of wisdom; toppling our tradition demands pride, the deadliest of the seven deadly sins. Where Saul

Alinsky enticed his readers to vice, the Gordon brothers encourage theirs to virtue.

President John F. Kennedy explained the difference half a century ago in the words of the socialist playwright George Bernard Shaw. "Some see things and say, 'Why?'" he explained. "But I dream things that never were, and I say, 'Why not?'" Kennedy's brother Robert adopted the line as a slogan for his own presidential campaign. Their other brother Edward quoted it at Robert's funeral, and generations of progressive politicians have parroted the line ever since. What Kennedy failed to mention is the specific origin of the quotation, which appears in Shaw's play *Back To Methuselah* in the mouth of the Serpent tempting Eve in the Garden of Eden. It is curious how often Satan crops up in the history of "progress."

Words such as "left" and "right," "forward" and "backward," "progress" and "regress" take a political discussion only so far; eventually the conversation must come to sin and grace because, as Cardinal Manning observed, "all human conflict is ultimately theological." The only real directions we can go are up to glory or down to perdition. If we hope to survive, we ought to take a step back and work out which way is which.

> Michael J. Knowles
> Los Angeles, CA
> 20 December 2019

Introduction

"Let priests take care not to accept from the liberal any ideas which, under the mask of good, pretend to reconcile justice with iniquity. Liberal Catholics are wolves in sheep's clothing. The priest must unveil to the people their perfidious plot, their iniquitous design. You will be called papist, clerical, RETROGRADE, intolerant. But pay no heed to the derision and mockery of the wicked. Have courage. You must never yield, nor is there any need to yield. You must go into the attack whole-heartedly, not in secret but in public, not behind barred doors, but in the open, in view of all."

—*Bishop Sarto (later Pope Pius X).*[1]

What exactly is a retrograde?

A retrograde is one of "God's spies," to borrow Shakespeare's term. A retrograde is a "deplorable 2.0"—the thinking man's version. A retrograde calculates, night and day, how to return to the Old World Order of moral and sexual decency, familial patriarchy, local rule and subsidiarity, classical masculinity and femininity, Christian liberty, republican sovereignty, national borders, faith and hope and charity,

---

[1]   Fr. Hieronymo Dal Gal, *St. Pius X: Life of the Beatus*, 1954.

goodness and beauty and truth, and most subtly and most importantly, the social kingship of Christ.

Recall Boromir of Gondor's words about reclaiming Osgiliath: "This city was once a jewel of our kingdom! A place of light and beauty and music. And so it shall be once more! Let the armies of Mordor know this: never again will the land of my people fall into enemy hands. The city of Osgiliath has been reclaimed for Gondor."[2]

Notwithstanding his eloquence, the retrograde is a devastatingly effective counterpuncher—with good reason.

In reference to the planned 2016 infiltration of the American Catholic Church by operatives connected to the Hillary Clinton presidential campaign, Republican Representative Paul Ryan reacted thus: "To despise the Catholic Church, accusing her of being 'seriously retrograde' [as Clinton's campaign did] is an insult to millions of people in this entire country."[3]

Representative Ryan was wrong: to be counted a "retrograde" by the radicals should be an honor worn on the lapels like a badge. In an era of profound spiritual and moral crisis like ours, the retrograde must joyfully cultivate the virtue of righteous fustiness. He must understand that in the trenches, laughter is war.

---

[2]   *The Lord of the Rings: The Two Towers*, extended ed. directed by Peter Jackson (New Line Cinema, 2002).

[3]   Alexandre Meyer, "Rivelazioni di WikiLeaks: lo staff della Clinton ha fomentato 'infiltrazioni' nella Chiesa Cattolica," Aleteia.org, October 17, 2016.

The retrograde has the unique capacity for understanding the discomfiture between the degenerate, radical-infiltrated world of decay on one side and the well-meaning but clueless Christian world on the other. The retrograde recognizes that the overwhelming majority of Christians today clearly have no interest in evangelizing the undecided world, which lies somewhere between Christianity and radicalism (usually naively favoring radicalism).

Under a shadow of such desolate and universal reach, becoming one of God's spies amounts to a last resort and a pure necessity. It involves not "deep cover," acting like the enemy, but rather "half cover," acting as a conservative "contra" in the secular arena. The retrograde is a crypto-Christian counterinsurgent willing to fight like a Navy Seal and to think like a counterintelligence officer.

Although these rules for retrogrades will never involve the commission of any intrinsic evil—violating any one of the Ten Commandments—the task is grim and gritty and not for the faint of heart. *In fact, this brief introduction will be one of the least subtle references to the book's religious reason for being.*

God's spies should adopt the mien of mixed martial arts hall of famer Bas Rutten and the mission of Father Gabrielle Amorth.

The following forty rules govern the retrograde program of attack, recovering then resuscitating the Christian West. Scattershot at first, the retrograde tends to a *rescue mission*, since, over the course of the last century, the West's "conservatives" were so entirely asleep at the wheel. Such "conservatives" over the last three generations have forfeited to radicals almost every inch of the landscape without a fight. It is nothing more than feckless cowardice masquerading as Christian charity. Initially, we must recover *whatever ground we can*. These forty rules should provide a brusque and, at times, abrupt start.

As our momentum in reclaiming the West grows, so too will our organizational principles sharpen. But for starters, the rules for retrogrades will deliberately involve action which—although calculated—will be blunt, non-surgical, and even artless in some places. The hour is late and the road before us is both winding and long. The fight ahead, that of re-Christianizing the neo-pagan West, will be ugly. It will be a war of attrition. We will fight with everything we have: our intellects, our hearts, and, if necessary, our bodies.

Retrogrades . . . to the streets: our aim is to reverse the deuced machinations of radicals like Saul Alinsky, who provided the inspiration for these rules by dedicating to Lucifer his *Rules for Radicals*.

Acknowledgment

Lest we forget to give a reverent acknowledgment to the very first retrograde: from Sacred Scripture and Tradition, the prince of the heavenly host who fought valiantly to preserve the Holy Name of God in the face of diabolical sacrilege, and who did it so effectively that he cast like lightning the Deceiver of the Whole World, Lucifer, and his cabal of demons from the heights of heaven into the pits of hell—St. Michael the Archangel.

Terms to Know

Alt-right: a neo-pagan, anti-Christian, racist political philosophy that is more aptly described as "alt-left." Virtually all retrogrades will be called "Alt-right" at some point, which is absurd since the core ideas of the latter are mostly leftist in nature. The Alt-right subscribes to radical ideas like eugenics, abortion, collectivism, Gnostic paganism, and identity politics. They are opportunely mischaracterized as "right wing" solely because their contentious, firebrand mien loosely resembles the belly-fire of the retrogrades. But look at our rules. These are creatures of the Left, first cousins to those radicals who seek to dissociate from the obvious political liability posed by their similarity with the Alt-right. The Alt-right stands for anti-retrograde principles in virtually every category (except for that of national sovereignty).

Baby Boomer: a group of people, born between 1946 and 1964, who lost every major cultural battle of their day to radicals, but who insist on dishing out smug, conventional advice and shaming the clear-thinkers who refuse to follow it.

Boomer-ism: a vapid, anti-intellectual, existentialist platitude that was taken to be infallible by the dope-smoking generation of the 1960s and 1970s but proves fallacious under even a small amount of scrutiny. Boomer-isms may *sound* profound but turn out to be uncommonly stupid new "folk sayings" about their radical new iterations of the "good life." Most often, they center upon the specious notion that life experience yields "higher" truths than those which can be known intellectually. Boomer-isms may also include human dispositions, presumptions, or reflexes; e.g., "if someone calls a non-racist, non-sexist person a 'racist' or a 'sexist,' he *must* yield his position." (The Baby Boomers figured this was the greatest devastation that a human could suffer.)

Calvinball: radicals' method of unilaterally controlling the rules of political engagement to arrive at a pre-ordained outcome, invariably favorable to the advancement of their radical interests. This term originates from the series, *Calvin and Hobbes*, wherein the eponymous main character, Calvin, keeps changing the rules and goals of a game to ensure his own victory.

Divisive Group Politics: radicals' system of political grievance-mongering and favoritism towards people of certain races, sexes, and other protected classes, which they use to curry favor with such groups in hopes of forming a large enough coalition to overthrow the old order of society.

Egalitarianism: the anti-Christian worldview which values distributive equality, or arithmetic proportion, over fairness, or geometric proportion. Egalitarians reject the Aristotelian definition of justice: give to each his due. Instead, they insist on giving to each the same amount, although it is not due. Egalitarianism lies at the root of most or all strains of utopianism because it insists on equality, against nature. Christianity condemns distributive or sexual egalitarianism as evil (with the exceptions of "equal dignity" and "equal opportunity," which accrue to all human beings).

Fragging, or **to frag:** the underhanded character assassination of one's own people. This expression is based on the historical term used to describe the killing of a fellow soldier by the detonation of a "fragmentation grenade," furtively attached to the unknowing soldier's pack. The term was used during the Vietnam War to describe actions by traitorous American soldiers. Infra, the term refers to non-radicals (sometimes including retrogrades) who sacrifice a retrograde so as not to appear unsavory to mainstream leftist outfits.

Militant Mod: a militant moderate. This non-discrete ideology includes either *pre-committed leftists unwilling to publicly own their inconvenient radicalism* or *subconsciously left-leaning moderates who obstinately refuse to be persuaded by the force of retrograde logic*. Both sorts of militant mod will customarily betray, if pushed hard enough, their underlying resentment for retrogrades and their quiet admiration for radicals.

Miyagi Complex: in the age of absconding fathers, referred to by Pope Benedict XVI as the crisis of fatherhood, this worldview presupposes that Western civilization is morally bankrupt. All moral mentors must therefore hail from Eastern civilization. The Miyagi Complex contemplates the truism that "everybody needs a sensei" to teach them *honor, self-discipline, integrity,* and other abstractions typically envisaged in Japanese characters at martial arts dojos, or in the tattooed iconography of the pseudo-profound.

Mod-Con: a moderate-conservative, or sometimes just a moderate. There exists only a marginal difference between the two non-discrete ideologies, such that they may be conceived as one. The mod-con is generally thought to comprise the majority of the non-insane persons in the twenty-first-century West. Mod-cons lack courage, care, or charisma. But they are often sincere, well-behaved denizens of Christendom who may be willing to be converted to retrogrades. Those who are reachable simply need the example of good retrograde leaders to carry them along.

Monolithic Boycott: the ineffectual, unpublished shadow banning of radical corporations by individual mod-cons, or sometimes, retrogrades. Often, conservatives will enact a "household policy" of refraining from the consumption of radical products, without understanding that boycotts only work when orchestrated with many others.

Political-Cultural War: the ideological battle between radicals and retrogrades for the soul of the West.

Radical: a progressive, Luciferian proponent of the anti-Christian New World Order who, in the words of Saul Alinsky, follows "the first radical known to man, who rebelled against the establishment and did it so effectively that he at least won his own kingdom—Lucifer."[4] The radical opposes everything true, good, and beautiful in this world, seeking to pervert, invert, and subvert it to achieve his darkling political agenda.

Retrograde: the dark knight of post-Christian Western civilization, frequently and unjustly blamed for his honorable repudiation of the New World Order built by radicals and brigands. The retrograde is, like Braveheart, an educated "savage who never lies." The retrograde works tirelessly to restore the Old World Order, seeking to imbue it with morality, decency, and most importantly, Christianity.

SJW: social justice warrior.

Woke: the state of being aware and angry about social "injustices" and "inequities," especially ones offensive to radical and progressive sensibilities.

---

4   Saul Alinsky, *Rules for Radicals*, 1971.

Rule 1

Always be on offense.

Generals know it; chess grandmasters know it; left-wing tacticians know it: to win a war, you need to be on offense. If you're content to rest on your laurels and play passive defense, you're eventually going to lose. Period. Perhaps General George Patton put it best: "No one ever won a war by going out and dying for his country; he won it by making some other dumb bastard die for *his* country."

In the long run, in terms of outcome, offense is always superior to defense. Offense benefits from momentum; defense only benefits from inertia. Inertia is static and can be overcome assuming that an actor summons sufficient force, which he is almost sure to do, given inertia's alluring static threshold. Offense also benefits from the inherent superiority of action as compared with reaction. In reaction, crucial time is lost in finding the proper response and executing it. Conversely, action, even where imprecisely directed or poorly executed, has the ability to do damage. Where a boxer throws an uppercut and lands it on his opponent, even if the more appropriate punch for the situation was a right cross, the uppercut still hurts and brings the boxer that much closer to a knockout win.

Moreover, offense is effective in increments, whereas defense is only effective in terms of end results. Imagine the game of football if the offense had an infinite number of downs (as opposed to the customary four) to score a touchdown. Eventually, the offense *will* score, even if it takes two hundred downs. The offense may throw an endzone-to-endzone pass and score in one play, or they may march the ball down the field with a series of choppy run plays, picking up three yards at a time. Either way, the offense is happy, since they get six points, and the defense is still dejected, since they're now losing the game. When you're on offense, you set the pace. If you remain on offense, you will (given sufficient time) accomplish your objectives.

It takes a dedicated effort to wrench the initiative away from an attacking opponent and put him on his heels, since humans don't possess the instinct to meet aggression with aggression. When a boxer is on the receiving end of a flurry of punches, he has the instinctive reaction to step back, put his eyes down, raise his guard, and cover up. However, to succeed at the highest levels, fighters need to learn to counterpunch, seizing the initiative by force. It's the same in the culture wars and politics. This is why Rahm Emmanuel infamously admonished fellow radicals, "You never want a serious crisis to go to waste. And what I mean by that [is] it's an opportunity to do things that you think you could not before." What Rahm was really saying is that liberals must *weaponize* current events so that the events redound to progressives' benefit. He's saying to seize the initiative by force and batter your opponent with an unending salvo of diverse shots. He's saying to use the environment to your advantage, to enable an attack. Tactically, he's spot-on.

So we retrogrades need to take back the initiative; we need to make a concerted effort to go on offense. After the next mass shooting, don't passively defend against the leftist media's mechanical, choreographed calls for "common-sense gun legislation" by pointing out that the proposed laws would do little to curb violence. Instead, put leftists on their heels by organizing a coordinated media blitz wherein commentators are instructed to hammer home the point that *crime rates are comparatively lower in regions where gun-ownership is higher.* Go on the offensive by challenging network hosts with questions like "Why are you against gun ownership when all the data suggests that it deters mass-shootings?" and "Why do you promote feminism and single-motherhood when you know that the overwhelming majority of mass-shootings are carried out by bitter fatherless young men?" If we want to end mass-shootings, we should encourage more people to carry firearms so that they can defend themselves. Organize a drive to subsidize guns for citizens in dangerous neighborhoods.

It's the same thing with abortion. When the pro-abortion lobby asks, "Why do you want to hurt women by depriving them of the right to choose?" don't give the usual pusillanimous, asinine conservative answer of "I want to help women by showing them that choosing life is always the best option." Instead, ask the smug leftist why he's fine with hurting girls in utero by allowing their mothers to have them dismembered and sucked from the womb, or boiled-alive in saline solution. Don't let radicals take up the mantle of being "pro-woman"; show how leftists hate women, as demonstrated by their indifference toward the millions of baby girls being slaughtered by mothers who are *literal* infanticidists.

If we want to win the culture wars, we have to craft the narrative ourselves—to content ourselves with passively responding to the left's cherry-picked and farcical narrative is suicidal. Train yourself to attack, work up your courage, and seize the day.

Rule 2

Conservatism is inherently Christian; intellectual conservatism is inherently Roman Catholic.

In America specifically, conservatism's guts have been Protestant, but its brains must be Catholic. It is true in Western civilization, generally. This is because Aristotle and St. Thomas Aquinas (together with the Christian Scripture and Tradition) informed the unique basis of all that's good in ancient and medieval Europe, which created Western culture. The retrograde needs to be aware of this and spread the message: the best of "American values" and "Western triumphalism" reduces to the teachings of Aristo-Thomism.

Aristotle lays out the *sine qua nons* for Western anthropology, justifying the interaction between man's free will, habit, virtue, politics, and culture. St. Thomas most aptly shows how Christian Tradition and Scripture perfected these Aristotelian building blocks of culture. "Goodies" like natural rights and limited government emanate uniquely from this source.

But in recent centuries, Aristotle and St. Thomas deliberately have been robbed of their due credit. On the right hand, the Reformation rejected this Aristo-Thomist basis for Western culture at the behest of *sola scriptura*; on the left hand, the Enlightenment made the same dismissal, except premised upon anti-Christian *scientism*. In other words, the two movements rejected Aristo-Thomism for opposite reasons.

Things played out interestingly in America. When their Protestant-Enlightenment worldview came up wanting, the American founders—and colonial and antebellum American culture—secretly drew (heavily!) on Aristo-Thomism while unabashedly denouncing Aristotle and Thomas. These two figures are basically the American retrograde's "dark knights," gathering all the undue blame and none of the due credit.

All republics live out a three-phase life cycle: first, *breaking the old regime*, and then *making the new regime*, and finally *staking the new regime in the culture*. Aristo-Thomism proves indispensable for all three phases. This is seen in American history specifically and in all republics generally.

Breaking the old regime: In 1776, the Declaration of Independence announced the breaking of the English rule over the American colonies. In the American republic—before it was even technically a republic—founders such as Thomas Jefferson and John Adams secretly drew on a Thomistic natural rights tradition[5] in the formulation and defense of the Declaration of Independence. Although the young colonies were

---

5   Thinkers like Robert Bellarmine and Protestant political thinkers who drew on Bellarmine and Aquinas.

peopled by Protestants outwardly hostile to Thom-
ism, the natural rights of the Declaration proved to be
unimaginable and incoherent without Thomas Aquinas's arrangement thereof.

Making the new regime: In 1787 and 1788, the draft-
ing and ratifying of the US Constitution memorialized
the making of the new American regime, premised
upon the violations of American rights enumerated in
the previous decade's Declaration. Framers of the US
Constitution like James Madison recognized that natural rights in republics were best secured by localism, a
principle derived from the Catholic concept of subsidiarity. Once again, this republican desideratum came
from the overlooked or maligned lineage of classical
thinkers such as Aristotle, Thomas Aquinas, Robert
Bellarmine, the Spanish theologians of the School
of Salamanca, and Montesquieu. Madison and the
framers called the concept "federalism," not subsidiarity, although it proves to be a simple Reformation-
Enlightenment reproduction thereof.

Staking the new regime in the culture: All the American founders and framers agreed that a good, new
Constitution accomplished nothing without implanta-
tion within a virtuous political culture. In other words,
the real life of a republic is lived after its foundational
documents have been ratified. The baton, as it were,
needed to be passed from 1770s revolutionaries and
1780s constitutionalists to the "everyday American" of
the 1790s and thereafter. Yet even within a Protestant citizenry, this required all the marks of a Catholic

people: virtue ethics in the populace, a Christian humanism based upon a sacramental order, a family economy, and a science and technology sector based upon Aristotelian realism. All these elements of culture required a Thomistic view of the human person, even as the young republic technically rejected the Church's insistence upon it.

While ecumenical conservative values can be broadly construed as "Christian," without contradiction, now busted is the tired old myth about the congruity between Puritan political acumen (which denies outright the possibility of liberty and virtue) and American values. The more specifically one wants and labors to ascribe American values to Protestantism, the more vigorously he must be rebuffed. This task falls to the retrograde: as he disabuses misinformed Americans of their political and cultural misconceptions, he replaces Puritanism with Aristo-Thomism as America's intellectual lodestar.

Finally, the retrograde must understand that small government can't be accomplished within a morally pluralistic society or over large land masses. Small government requires small spaces with alert, active, virtuous retrograde-citizens prepared to "organize themselves" in an equal and opposite way to the demands of Saul Alinsky.

Rule 3

No truth is "off-limits"; we must never be ashamed to be candid.

Radicals have successfully convinced many mod-cons to self-censor, insisting that some truths are "too offensive" to be spoken in decent society. They've thus driven the retrograde message underground, forcing us to whisper in darkness a host of medicinal truths deserving of the limpid radiance of day. Should retrogrades continue to submit to such treacherous advice, we are destined to be routed in our fight for the soul of society. We know, on the highest authority, that apart from being desirable for its own sake, the truth shall set mankind free. And, thus, it is to be pursued at all costs. If sheepish mod-cons neglect to fiercely and openly denounce the perversities that radicals are attempting to usher in, radicals will triumph by default. Darkness can only prevail when men of good will are made afraid to light a candle.

It is of paramount importance to remember that *acts of the intellect always precede acts of the will.* In other words, before we act for a certain end, the intellect, consciously or not, must decide that such an end is the "good," the object most worthy of our pursuit. No one sets out to achieve what he views as an inferior or bad end. Thus, in order to win the culture, we must boldly and loudly speak truth so our fellow men can first recognize what is verily good and, subsequently, firmly set their wills on achieving it. If something is true, then we have a duty to say it so that society will be built on a foundation of rock instead of a foundation of sand.

Be reminded that there is no such thing as an intrinsically hateful truth; motive is always a deciding factor in analyzing the morality of a seemingly harsh statement. Sometimes charity and prudence dictate that one should even call his own mother "fat": perhaps she is a diabetic or has heart disease and hearing such a hard truth will allow her to reformulate her diet and add years to her life. More important yet, perhaps she is a glutton needing chastisement against a habituated mortal sin. Similarly, we do no one any favors when we, out of fear of being slandered as "racist," "sexist," "jingoist," "homophobic," "intolerant," or "hateful," (or any other empty radical scare-words) consent to hide the light of unpopular truths under a bushel basket. When we fail to acknowledge sensitive truths (e.g., that contemporary American black fatherlessness is linked with their disproportionately high crime rates; that single motherhood is ruinous for children; that unchecked immigration is undermining the fabric of American culture; that homosexual relations are vile, depraved, hateful acts; that men can't actually become women and vice versa), we short-change our fellow man, since we deprive him of the opportunity to reform his life to bring it into harmony with right order. Hard sayings must be shouted loudly, for the benefit of all mankind—damn the consequences. Moreover, if retrogrades band together and resolve to be undeterred in our vocalization of unpopular truths, it will be impossible for big media and big business to ostracize us. The corporate goons in human resources won't be able to fire all of us. It's impossible to effectively silence such a significant segment of the population.

The story of *the Emperor's New Clothes* serves as an uncannily apropos allegory for modern man's affinity for shrinking from his duty to proclaim truth. In the fable, the emperor is duped by two shysters into purchasing imaginary clothes so that when he "gets dressed" in his new "attire," in reality, he's naked. Despite the fact that the emperor is humiliating himself by strutting around the town square in a full state of undress, none of the emperor's men or townspeople, for fear of appearing foolish or insolent, will speak out to tell the emperor that his wardrobe is a fraud. The people uniformly tickle the emperor's ear, complimenting his splendid linens and refined sartorial taste. Except one little boy. One little boy, out of the whole town, sees the emperor and, with umbrage in his voice, exclaims, "But the emperor isn't wearing any clothes. He's naked!" In the aftermath of this one child's naïve candor, the people come to their senses and soberly admit the obvious: truly, the emperor is not wearing any clothes.

The weakness of mankind is such that the majority are content to go along with a lie out of fear of blowback should they stand and fight for truth. It's a somber realization that most people are consequentialists who would rather pretend a naked emperor is dressed in fine linen rather than risk looking foolish— or worse yet, risk a stint in the dungeon. At the same time, we should take solace that a lone voice (even that of a child) bravely crying out in the wilderness is often sufficient to call men to their senses, to call men away from mass delusion. Be the lone voice in your locale, and soon we will marshal a network of woke retrogrades, ready to turn the tides of a war we've long been losing. The only precondition for the death of the Gospel is silence. Never be cowed. Always speak truth, especially when it's unpopular. Hold fast to the musings of George Washington: "I hope I shall possess firmness and virtue enough to maintain what I consider the most enviable of all titles, the character of an honest man."

Rule 4

Egalitarianism is evil: the retrograde must loudly announce that Christian teaching and nature are generally anti-egalitarian.

This applies to both *marital* (sexual) and *distributive* (economic) relations. Christianity formally rejects all types of utopianism, usually predicated on egalitarianism. In short, it is unnatural—even anti-natural—to expect, as today's popular culture does, a uniformity of roles and talents among human beings.

Forced equality bears wicked fruits. As such, we should reject the notion of "gender neutral language," "participation trophies," ties in ball games, and measures toward perfectly equal incomes among households. Instead, we should insist upon gender-specific grammar, trophies only for champions, tiebreakers in sports, and a meritocratic economy which guarantees to each his due. Only these are truly Christian and aligned with natural law.

Radicals have recently changed the world by crying out "diversity, diversity!" while simultaneously condemning all forms of non-egalitarianism. This is a bold contradiction. But it has heretofore gone unnoticed, or at least unannounced, by retrogrades. Truly healthy diversity is achieved by the widespread

cultural acknowledgement of a talented "natural aris-
toi" (as Thomas Jefferson noted) and its opposite
(i.e., a less talented average citizen). The retrograde
announces the following economic fact of life: certain
sorts are more talented, bigger, faster, and better than
others. Along similar lines, men and women comprise natural opposites. Egalitarianism is evil because
it denies these basic truths of nature.

Of course, two exceptional forms of modified
equality *do* qualify as Christian: equality of *dignity* and
of *opportunity*, exceptions in the Christian arenas of
matrimony and political economy, respectively. First,
let's examine "equality" in the realm of matrimony.
Men and women are naturally, unalterably disparate.
By now, radicals have used the slippery concept of
equality to justify the near-total destruction of matrimony. Sexual equality (even more than its economic
sibling) proves to be a juggernaut, engulfing everything it touches.

The retrograde understands that men and women
are not at all equals: *men are superior at being male,
as women are superior at being female.* The Christian
doctrine of complementarity involves equality in *dignity* between men and women but not in function or
power. As a term of art, dignity stands for the proposition that all human beings—every man and woman
alike—enjoy rights in the eyes of God on account of
their immortal souls. Yet dignity does not accrue from
merit or usefulness. On the other hand, sexual roles
and talents have quite a lot to do with merit when

we consider the functioning of the efficient household economy: men were built to do some things and women were built to do others.

Accordingly, even universal human rights (e.g., life or liberty) pertain and accrue to the two sexes differently. The manner in which men and women spend their rights should be expected to vary. In fact, men and women prove to be complementary precisely *because* of the natural disparity of function and power between them. A husband admires his wife's grace, as she admires his efficacy.[6]

Everything of a sexual nature after the 1960s grew monochromatic, uniform, and bland. Radicals violated their own claimed admiration of diversity, suggesting across all cultural venues that neither the male set of qualities—power, assertion, and activity—nor the female set—fealty, gentleness, and receptivity— turn out to be sex-specific. Through lies, force, and

---

[6]   The natural force that arises in that space of inter-sexual admiration may only be described as *attraction*, a beautiful phenomenon that cannot exist without male-female differences. The natural law ensures that, on account of stark sexual differences of body and soul, men and women have indispensably different roles to play. Thus are they drawn to one another. Women are attracted to the strength, assertiveness, and activity of good men; men are attracted to the fealty, gentleness, and receptivity of good women. Along those lines, males attract females through leadership, just as females attract males through fealty. Natural complementarity dictates a beautiful "fit" between men and women. At least, this was the case before radicals began attempting to pervert human sexuality in the popular mind: they did so by equalizing the sexes (or claiming to have done so).

cajoling, radicals convinced most people that *culture, not nature,* fabricated the sexual differences commonly observed prior to the sexual revolution. In other words, radicals popularized the lie that nature does not lay out "gender roles." Sexual equality was their primary means of leveling the landscape: women should become soldiers and pretend to like it; men should become doddering wet nurses and pretend to like it.

Like all utopian visions, sexual equality created an actual dystopia, a hell on earth. The retrograde seeks to undo this. Through truth, forceful reasoning, and cajoling, retrogrades must reverse this sweeping cultural lie by showing the *joy* of the disparity between the two sexes, especially in the form of healthy marriages. Our mutual differences make men and women natural partners: they make us see and appreciate one another's strengths, which are not sex-fungible.

Strangely enough, much of the retrograde's logic regarding the complementarian rapport between the two sexes applies with equal rigor to just economics (in a less sexy way): in the economic case, the radicals attacked the merit which generates natural economic diversity. As Pope Leo XIII reminds his reader in warning against the new socialist reconfiguration of the mutual relationship between workers and their bosses, "each needs the other: capital cannot do without labor, nor labor without capital."[7] The

---

[7]   *Rerum Novarum,* 19.

great pope goes on to specify the danger: "To remedy these wrongs the socialists, working on the poor man's envy of the rich, are striving to do away with private property, and contend that individual possessions should become the common property of all, to be administered by the State or by municipal bodies. They hold that by thus transferring property from private individuals to the community, the present mischievous state of things will be set to rights, inasmuch as each citizen will then get his fair share of whatever there is to enjoy."[8]

Once more, egalitarianism is evil, Pope Leo XIII reminds us. On the contrary, he makes it clear that in a robust and just political economy with reasonably fair conditions, "what you reap is what you sow."

Pope Leo wrote one of the most important encyclicals of all time simply by channeling the basic anti-egalitarian attitudes of Aristotle and Thomas Aquinas. According to Aristotle, fairness (or "distributive justice") honors proportion: "for if persons are not equal, they ought not have equal shares."[9] More specifically, fairness honors *geometrical* proportion: unequal shares for unequal merit. Conversely, equality haphazardly "honors" what Aristotle calls *arithmetic* proportion—equal shares for unequal merit—but Aristotle deems that such egalitarianism violates justice. Thomas Aquinas, for his part, agrees: "If property

---

8   *Rerum Novarum*, 4.
9   Aristotle, *Nicomachean Ethics,* V, iii, 7-8.

were equalized among the households, . . . it would lead to a corruption of the polity. It also follows that the equalization of possessions is unsuitable from a consideration of the gradation of personages, as well as from human nature. There is a difference between citizens just as there is between members of a body. . . . The virtue and function of different members is different."[10]

The retrograde knows that in actuality there were *two*, not *one*, socialist "errors of Russia" warned against at Fatima in 1917: sexual egalitarianism and economic egalitarianism. The West has succumbed to both, although moderate right-wingers have usually picked one side or the other to spend energy in countering.[11] *Both* egalitarian errors of Russia must be undone, however. *Both* must be decried and defeated in the West. Retrogrades have been appointed by the late hour to be the soldiers fighting to the death this two-front war.

---

[10]   Thomas Aquinas, *De Regimine Principium*, Book 4, Ch. 9, p. 76.

[11]   As shown clearly by the "Melee at CUA" debate on 9/5/19 between David French and Sohrab Ahmari, both types of non-retrograde conservative—post-liberals and classical liberals—have chosen to combat one but not both types of Russia's errors.

Rule 5

Risus bellum est: laughter is war.

The only possible response by a sane man to an insane claim is laughter and ridicule. Never buy radical premises. In the course of political badinage, do not settle for reason where action is due (and vice versa). This logic extends with especial force to the needfulness of the scornful guffaw. Laugh openly at your radical opponent's insane, constant recusals of the Christian West.

With good reason, the expression, "I will not dignify that claim with a response," bears profound value against radicals, especially in the clownish cultural and political scene today. The act of laughing makes for a devastating weapon of cultural war because there is simply no dignified reply to it!

If a man responds line-item to a radical's insane proposition in a way which suggests that it deserves more dignity than it actually merits, moderate and incautious listeners nearby may be persuaded in the wrong direction. If they are not persuaded *all the way* in the wrong direction, they will at the very least lose interest in the prolix dialogue between you and the radical, assuming as they walk away that the truth is probably something of a median between the two positions they heard. On the other hand, if they had heard you simply laugh at the idiotic blasphemy leveled by the radical, your punchy laughter would have well served both their curiosity and their short attention span.

In other words, one need not outsmart oneself by avoiding the intuitive schoolyard approach of ridicule. Trust your gut, especially when it tells you to laugh at radical claims. Retrogrades who fail to respond with laughter will end up, in good faith, buying dangerous premises that would have more easily been rejected by simple ridicule in the first place. Not only does this needlessly lengthen what should be quick, pithy "conversations" with radicals, but more importantly, it lends false credibility to incredible and neurotoxic ideas (even in the shrewd mind of the retrograde).

The conventional wisdom by old-guard types within the ranks of "humble" Christianity or center-right politics would be either to listen "compassionately" without reply or to "reason it out" slowly in dialogue. Both of these replies are gravely mistaken, which costs their users efficacy and "street cred." The latter is earned by satisfying the gut instincts.

For example, the proposition that "men have penises" is now supposed to be controversial. Radical haters of the Christian "patriarchy" have seen to it that the most fundamental Christian teachings on human sexuality—and pretty much everything else—are now received as dubious and hateful. This represents abject madness.

Listening compassionately to a confused person of this persuasion is never a bad idea *in the one-on-one context*. But a retrograde, as we said above, is exceedingly unlikely to find himself in private dialogues with transsexuals. Dialogue will usually be of the public sort. Accordingly, some form of winsome public reply will be needed. Don't borrow trouble; take shortcuts where they present themselves. The derisive laugh will not be available for all the vast array of radical claims, many of which will have to be forensically dispelled. But where laughter is sufficient, use it!

Any thoughtful—or even unthoughtful—reply (aside from scornful laughter) tendered to a radical who attempts to rebut the obvious fact that only "men have penises," will automatically ennoble the inane notion that natural sexuality can be altered. Replying with diligently collected biological data, of course, might winsomely convince an interlocutor who honestly didn't already know this basic fact of human life. But since there are virtually zero honest disbelievers in the fact of two biological sexes, your data (and the time you spent to acquire it) will have been misspent on fools.

Retrogrades' time-efficiency and individual reputations will improve sharply upon the habituation of the well-timed, well-placed guffaw of unmuted derision.

Rule 6

Never compromise with radicals on their initiatives.

Radicals work to implement the progressive agenda in increments. (We can thus call their method "incrementalism.") There are a couple reasons for this. Were radicals to impose their disordered world-view all at once, it would prove so unnatural and dystopian that it would forever shatter the common man's perception of progressivism as a viable political philosophy. Since many of the ideas of radicals are so far out of the mainstream of Western convention, to avoid backlash, their ideas must be introduced slowly and methodically so as to gradually acclimate people to the brave new world, desensitizing them to its bitterness. Moreover, to hoodwink opposing political parties and to circumvent political resistance, radicals must advance their ideas slowly, till such time as they achieve a critical mass, a tipping point at which their perverse ideas have taken root in the hearts and minds of the voting populace. Only then can their endgame, their true vision, be revealed, insulated from the hazard of political consequence.

Because incrementalism is at the nucleus of radicals' blueprint for capturing the culture, and because radicals are, at this point, the active principle driving cultural change, compromising on disputed issues invariably works in their favor. Consider, for instance, a debate on raising taxes. Let's imagine that a radical lawmaker floats the idea of a 90 percent federal income tax rate for top wage earners in order to ameliorate a budget deficit. Imagine, too, that one of the radical lawmaker's "moderate" confreres retorts that a 90 percent income tax is unreasonable and proposes a "mere" 50 percent income tax. After some haggling, perhaps the lawmakers decide to compromise and agree on a 70 percent income tax rate for top earners. Suppose now that, in ensuing years, irresponsible government spending yields yet another deficit. The same radical lawmaker, as is his habit, will again propose raising taxes in an effort to cure the deficit. Again, he will float the 90 percent income tax number. Again, the radical's "moderate" confrere will balk at the 90 percent figure, but wanting to be "reasonable" and address the looming deficit, the moderate will this time propose splitting the difference and bringing the income tax rate up to a more palatable 80 percent rate. Should this cycle of punctuated creep be allowed to continue over time, the radical will eventually taste the 90 percent rate he had been clamoring for all along. While he could not have succeeded in having his demands met at first, by working in increments, by appearing reasonable and settling for a series of upward-ascending compromises, the radical has ultimately prevailed. A series of compromises inevitably leads to the active party achieving total victory, since with each successive compromise, the end goal is brought that much nearer.

It should also be noted that radicals habitually use ground gained in previous victories as launching points for future attacks. When they make inroads through compromise, they use their forward momentum to springboard themselves to further conquests. Consider the issue of women clergy. Radicals can't simply demand that women immediately assume roles as high ranking prelates in the Church—they'd be laughed out of town; such a change would be too drastic an overhaul, too severe a breach with timeless tradition to merit serious consideration. And radicals know this all too well. So they take a more cunning tack to achieve their goal: they complain that women are "underrepresented in the Church" and that, in order to fully make use of women's "surplus talents," they "need more access to even modest positions of leadership and responsibility." As such, radicals may propose that women should have access to lower clerical positions—to the diaconate, perhaps. And if in an ill-conceived attempt to sate feminist lust for power, the Church were to try to accommodate such demands and indulge radical women by appointing them deaconesses, it would be only a matter of time before radicals pointed to the deaconesses that had achieved a certain amount of renown or stature and pointedly inquire, "Why, since these women have fulfilled their lower clerical duties with such distinction and aplomb, should they be prohibited from acquiring the office of priestess?" Pressing their advantage, they would put the Church on the spot by asking the very questions whose unseemly answers were the impetus for its initial capitulation. In pressing their advantage in this way, radicals would continue to gain ground at an exponentially increasing pace. If this pattern were allowed to continue unabated, given the passage of enough time, eventually women would attain the papacy.

Radicals rely on incrementalism, and incrementalism thrives on a system of compromise. Hence, the retrograde must never compromise with the radical on a disputed issue; he must steadfastly refuse to give ground, gnashing his teeth before budging an inch. In this way, we can blunt the advance of radicalism, and begin to make our own headway in the culture wars.

Rule 7

Never let radical mischief go unpunished.
(Make a stink about everything.)

Mod-cons are habitually cowardly and lazy, but they fancy themselves magnanimous, charitable, and wise. Whitewashing their indifferentism and chronic failure to react to grievous insults as "stateliness" and "poise" and "being the bigger man," and all sorts of other delirious euphemisms, mod-cons have afforded radicals so much leniency in deportment and speech that radicals now believe that they can say and do anything to a retrograde without fear of reproach. It is this abdication of the duty to counterpunch that has allowed the conduct of radicals to devolve to its current critical level of vile coarseness. It is this abdication of the duty to well with righteous anger that has enabled the Antifa mob to run amok through large portions of various urban areas, committing batteries on innocent passersby with impunity. It is this abdication of the duty to defend our honor that has relegated those not on board with radical propaganda to *de facto* second-class-citizen status.

Radicals have successfully handed down to Western society an unofficial but despotic code of conduct.

They have shuttered our ability to speak truth freely; they have set forth rules dictating what sorts of things we may joke about without running afoul of the thought police; they've narrowed our styles of dress and personal adornment by admonishing us about "cultural appropriation"; they've dictated the proper "ratio" for women and minority appearances in movies and television; they've twisted our arms to make us pretend that men who grow out their hair, shave their Adam's apples, speak with a phony lisp, and wear gaudy dresses are actually women. And the way that radicals have been able to get society to accede to their fell new code of conduct is by grievance-mongering: they gripe, complain, and take offense about *everything* that doesn't conform to their bizarre sensibilities. But not only do they gripe, complain, and take offense, they also call corporate offices, write letters to congress, picket businesses, and threaten boycotts. In fact, they have special institutions like the "Corporate Accountability Project" dedicated to policing whether businesses are sufficiently "woke," or if they need to be cudgeled into compliance with the new code of conduct.

Radicals' reactionary impulse, along with their assiduous commitment to following their initial umbrage with tangible demands for redress (often at the point of an economic bayonet), is the reason that we feel a subconscious pang of guilt when we say something true but politically incorrect; it's the reason that all burglars in home security commercials *have* to be

Caucasian (despite the fact that blacks and Hispanics have a much higher crime rate per capita); it's the reason that in crime shows, hotshot lawyers at top law firms are reliably depicted as being sassy women (despite the fact that the overwhelming number of top law firm partners are men); it's the reason we have to call Bruce Jenner "Caitlyn"; it's the reason we have to pretend fat women make suitable fashion models; it's the reason we have to pretend that rap and graffiti are art; it's the reason that we have to pretend that wives, and not husbands, are the heads of households.

Retrogrades need to reassert *our* fighting spirit. When we witness an injustice, when we see a serious breach of decorum or decency, when marketing departments choose to make us the butt of their jokes, we need to get *mad*, and we need to actualize the potential energy of our initial anger into hot, messy kinetic energy by protesting, writing letters, making phone calls, and organizing non-monolithic boycotts. For too long have we abided white men being universally portrayed on television as fat, stupid, subservient slobs; for too long have we tolerated razor companies that scold men for "toxic masculinity"; for too long have we allowed major retailers to peddle "slutty nun" costumes in the run-up to Halloween; for too long have we watched an NFL that mandates that grown men wear pink to raise money for a disease that primarily affects women; for too long have we let Tide commercials show emasculated housedads doing laundry on weekdays while their careerist wives are at work; for too long have we let Antifa bully old women; for too long have we allowed unfunny, loud-mouthed comediennes to celebrate abortion publicly and cut the head off of Trump effigies; for too long have we patronized anti-American Hollywood movies and award shows; for too long have we financed an NBA that boycotts states because they don't let psy-chologically unstable and sexually confused men use women's restrooms; for too long have we let homo-sexual depravity be thrust in our faces in commercials and sitcoms. Tolerate this abuse no longer. As Dylan Thomas exhorts, "Do not go gentle into that good night."

It's time to get mad and resolve ourselves to pun-ishing radical mischief. Verbally chastise wrongdoers; seek to get those who use employment positions to advance radicalism fired from their jobs; flood cus-tomer feedback centers with letters and negative reviews. Do *anything*, and do it loudly and with aplomb; but most of all, stop doing nothing. The only way to stop a bully is by punching him in the mouth. Hard.

Rule 8

**It is a damnable lie that humility disallows
Christians from standing up (for what they
believe) in the cultural and political forum!**

The requirements of Christian piety do not include
the forfeiture of hallowed ground to the Jacobins.
On the contrary, humility and piety require the God-
fearing defense of culture. One humbly submits oneself to the crusade.

In reality, humility explicates a certain *disposition*,
not a certain *act* (as Aristotle wrote of all virtue): prudence, not humility, governs the Christian exigencies
of forming "real time" daily rejoinders to the radical
enemies of culture and civil order. If anything, true
humility *empowers* retrogrades to fight evil in their
midst. In other words, we are allowed (and in many
cases, even obligated) to fight back, if necessary, in
word and in deed.

Many cowardly Christian men on the right wing
have made from their quietude a comfortable, unchal-
lenged life for themselves. Through a cleverly perverted sense of Christian humility, such men have
unabashedly popularized their habitual submission
to radicals. They even presume to lecture American

retrogrades about the "virtues" of their own complacent acts of pusillanimity: "We must suffer the slings
and arrows of this world in stoicism," they say as they
profit in peace, dodging any real suffering, while the
rest of us fight. What they're really avoiding is the
suffering itself.

To be sure, such phony conservatives have acquit-
ted themselves very poorly in the defense of Western
civilization because they don't care much for it, *except
in what it can do for them.* And this attitude reflects
the opposite of humility. This attitude is really self-
service and cowardice dressed up in the moral garb
of bourgeois Christianity, fake Christianity. This rationalization has grown in popularity to the extent that
many earnest retrogrades ask, "Is resisting evil with
good . . . evil?" Of course not! We respond to those
who have characterized metaphorical *draft-dodging*
as *brave humility* with Isaiah 5:20: "Woe to those who
call evil good and good evil, who put darkness for
light and light for darkness, who put bitter for sweet
and sweet for bitter!"

Also, recall the sage advice of St. Jerome: "Nothing
is more to be feared than too long a peace. You are
deceived if you think that a Christian can live without persecution. He suffers the greatest persecution
of all who lives under none. A storm puts a man on
his guard and obliges him to exert his utmost efforts
to avoid shipwreck." Note Jerome's spiked words of
alarm, which fustily enjoin the Christian to put up his

guard and to spend his utmost efforts on the fight. St. Jerome invokes neither pacifism nor passivism.

Finally, recall St. Augustine's admonition: "Hope has two beautiful daughters; their names are Anger and Courage. Anger at the way things are, and Courage to see that they do not remain as they are." In actuality, the phony conservatives who mischaracterize cowardice as humility frequently number among the militant mods who would speak out more loudly against retrogrades than radicals. The pious, affected quietude of these Judases is frequently pierced—by their own traitorous voices—in order to distance themselves from retrogrades. Indeed, the radical imbalance currently plaguing the West has benefitted more parties than just the radicals themselves! It works to the benefit of the silent, copacetic Christians who profit from their own non-interference in radical machinations. And this is an ugly fact, in the grand scheme of things.

In short, pacifism is not humility. Humility constitutes one's attitude at the end of the day, when one hits one's knees in prayer or when the head hits the pillow. But it does not require a retrograde to submit to evil. As Thomas Aquinas points out, humility renders the spirit strong, not weak. Lastly, St. Jose María Escrivá wrote, "Unless you mortify yourself, you'll never become a prayerful soul." For gentle-fibered men who would rather be silent than fight, the best means of self-mortification may just be to enter the fray!

Rule 9

Control of language is control of thought; don't let radicals control the language.

Let me take this opportunity to invert a pompous Marxist aphorism: language (as opposed to religion) is the true opiate of the masses. It is for this reason that a calling-card of tyrannical regimes throughout history has been their inclination to cloak their true despotic natures in the disarming nomenclature of enlightened, urbane, first-world, free societies.

Dystopian dictatorships habitually employ language that superficially calls to mind the benevolent governments of Western civil society: the Union of Soviet Socialist Republics, the Democratic People's Republic of (North) Korea, the People's Republic of China, the (East) German Democratic Republic, and Democratic Kampuchea are but a few examples. Each of these states is or was a smoldering beacon of hell on earth. But by invoking universally desirable governmental attributes like "representation," "democracy," "populism," and "republic" in the appellations of their respective states, Machiavellian autocrats have placated their gullible subjects through sheer power of suggestion. Retrogrades must learn from the mistakes of history; we must concertedly resist the slow poison of lingual manipulation. The manipulation of language is, at its core, the manipulation of people.

Lexical trickery is not limited to tin-pot dictatorships. Quite the contrary, it is a tactic employed by radicals of all stripes. Radicals are well aware that if they were to do intellectual battle with free-market, natural-rights conservatives on a level academic playing field, they'd be thoroughly humiliated—quickly checkmated by the cruel hand of unshackled reason. Thus, to borrow from Captain Jack Sparrow, that doesn't give liberals much incentive to "fight fair," does it? After all, "facts are stubborn things" that speak volumes if left unmolested by deceitful party lines. Since radicalism is wrong in both its presuppositions and conclusions, its recent palpable successes can only have followed on the heels of radicals' success in controlling our language and discourse.

Examples of radicals' lingual tampering are legion. Brutally slaughtering and dismembering babies in utero is now lauded as "women's reproductive rights"; illegal aliens are now "undocumented workers"; the judicial redefinition of marriage to include deviant sodomitical unions is "marriage equality"; workplace and educational sex-based favoritism has become "women's advancement"; disarming law-abiding citizens is now praised as "common sense gun regulation"; Muslims beheading people in the name of Allah is "workplace violence"; the most violent religion on earth is the "religion of peace"; anti-Christian bigotry masquerades as "the separation of Church and state"; indoctrinating six-year-olds with homosexual and transsexual filth is an "anti-bullying campaign"; and government theft through unfairly staggered tax brackets is "having the rich pay their fair share." Right-speak predominates in these Orwellian times.

To draw upon a few of the foregoing examples, we can confidently state that Planned Parenthood wouldn't be long for this world if it had to publicly acknowledge, rather than mask, the fact that its business model revolves around child-assassination. Fewer people would balk about deporting immigrants if they understood them to be criminally present in the United States. If radicals had to admit that homosexuals have always had the right to marry (a person of the opposite sex), it would be more difficult for them to rationalize the whimsical redefinition of a timeless institution. There would be a dearth of "gender dysphoric," synthetic-hormone guzzling, nine-year-olds running around if we could only admit that it's virtuous to be repulsed by hairy, female-impersonating men wearing lipstick and gowns. Thus, for radicals, facts such as these must be circumvented with mendacious euphemisms if they are to win over the average American. It falls on retrogrades to push back against the lingual manipulation of radicals, refusing to have our vocabulary dictated to us.

Another front in radicals' war on word usage is that of "gender-neutral language." As with radicals' policing of what passes for acceptable vocabulary, we must resist rewriting the English language so that it conforms to feminist sensibilities. One component of the gender-neutral language theater that is particularly deserving of our attention is the use of "inclusive" pronouns. It is (and always has been) proper to use the masculine pronouns "he," "him," and "his" when referring to a generic person, or to a person of unknown sex (since English does not have a third-person singular gender-neutral pronoun). In precise writing and speaking, all gender-neutral alternatives to the masculine third-person pronoun are "to be shunned" as they represent nothing short of the sheer torture of the English language.[12] Nevertheless, a great deal of lobotomized, neutered mod-cons bend over backwards to use unwieldy politically-correct phrases like "he or she," "his or hers," "s/he," or the cringe-worthy "they" when speaking of a singular third person, to avoid seeming "chauvinistic." By capitulating to radicals' bowdlerization of the English language, we implicitly concede that the critique of "latent sexism" in the language is meritorious, whether we mean to convey assent or not.

Language matters. A lot. And radicals are highly cognizant of this. If we continue to cede control of the English language to scoldy, imperious SJWs; then we might as well just officially surrender Western society to them, as a *fait accompli*. Stand your ground. Use

---

12   Theodore M. Bernstein, *The Careful Writer: A Modern Guide to English Usage* (New York: Atheneum, 1977), 351.

the words that most faithfully describe a concept, not the unwieldy, hyphenated euphemism that the radical would prefer because it tends to paint his agenda in a positive light. Conserve the rules of our language, and don't capitulate when radicals attempt to change them to conform to the asinine presumptions of "critical theory." Language is a tool for communicating truth. If language is manipulated, then truth is manipulated.

Rule 10

Radicals, who manipulate language, must be beaten at their own game, and then in many other venues as well—decisively, definitively, and mercilessly.

After all, we strive against the "powers and principalities." The retrograde's fight involves the reclamation of the aching West from the furious clutches of devils; more importantly still, the fight is waged for the very souls of bystanders and moderates.

So use a little showmanship. Make it a spectacle to behold. Beat a radical in a debate—look good doing it—and then challenge him to a boxing match. The former contest wins minds; the latter wins hearts. You never know whether a listener will be converted by heart or mind first, meaning that both approaches are needful. The retrograde can afford to neglect neither. At this late hour, retrogrades need victories across multiple venues. If, for example, a smug radical talk show host challenges a "square" conservative senator to a public one-on-one basketball game, or vice versa, it is insufficient to the task that the senator beats the talk show host by a score of 15–14. This is actually a loss, not a victory: consult history, if the reader fails to believe it.[13]

A marginal victory in a symbolic basketball game of this sort amounts to a nullity, or worse. Will anyone remember a less than heroic victory by the senator over the mouthy talk show host? Negative. A forgettable performance is a regrettable performance because it leaves the retrograde in the same position he was in before, except he looks dogged and overwrought in the effort spent. The only true victory is a stark one, with public contests of this sort—which are the ultimate manner of demonstrating to both types of moderate that retrogrades are *anything but* the uninteresting, untalented, unidimensional Puritans they've taken us to be. On the contrary, retrogrades must be cultivated savages, with the motto from *Braveheart*: *Ego nunquam pronunciari mendacium! Sed ego sum homo indomitus.*

But again, in order to prove this to anybody, you have to win and win handsomely. In order to do that, you've got to be sitting on talent aside from "book smarts." The need for "landslide" victories also goes for boxing matches (one of my favorite alternatives to verbal forensics), footraces, spelling contests, chess matches, ring tosses, poker tournaments, geography bees, et cetera. Although it may be puerile, it is also rather *classical* to resolve otherwise irreconcilable

---

[13]   Ted Cruz vs. Jimmy Kimmel public basketball game on June 16, 2018.

ideological differences—in the public arena any-way—with some other praiseworthy and manly met-ric. Since the days of the Ancient Greeks, certain types of contest (between two parties making adverse claims) have proven relevant to the public.

Such contests turn out to be alternative ways of showing the world—or even just radical family members back home for the holidays—the manly and vir-tuous merits of the retrograde worldview, the darkling genius of Christendom. Most people are readier to cede personal respect than intellectual respect. Even my liberal students are willing to listen to one of my lectures after they've seen me handle a basketball. The true retrograde is a force majeure, out to show the world the midnightly strength of the righteous man—a cultivated savage and a principled conqueror. Again, his motto is that of William Wallace, cited above: "I never lie! But I am a savage!" Or failing that, the retrograde may just be the principled *mentor* to a conqueror, in the case of the teacher of Alexander the Great (and student of Plato), Aristotle. Aristotle is the mack daddy and godfather of all polymath-retrogrades, whose many Western-civilization-forg-ing fields of expertise included physics, metaphysics, poetry, theater, music, logic, rhetoric, politics, ethics, biology, and zoology.

The "men of '76," America's retrograde revolution-ary-founders, *needed to be* comprised largely of poly-maths for the simple reason that backward-looking revolutions require loyal throngs of followers, necessitating charismatic chieftains—men of many parts and maestros of multiple simultaneous talents. American retrograde Thomas Jefferson, a polyglot (fluent in Greek, Latin, French, Spanish, Italian, and German), was also a polymath: "agriculturalist, anthropologist, architect, astronomer, bibliophile, botanist, classicist, diplomat, educator, ethnologist, farmer, geographer, gourmet, horseman, horticulturist, inventor, lawyer, lexicographer, linguist, mathematician, meteorologist, musician, naturalist, numismatist, paleontologist, philosopher, political philosopher, scientist, statesman, violinist, writer."[14] It takes this sort of multi-venue genius to take down a statist empire.

The greater the retrograde's task at hand, the more needful of polymathic genius. And in 2019, restoring America to her former wisdom and beauty requires as many moral, intellectual, physical geniuses as can be mustered from among our ranks. There's no time for sitting passively on the couch. Retrogrades to your training stations!

---

[14]   https://jeffersonia.wordpress.com/2009/01/06/6/.

Rule 11

Never trust a man who is unwilling to have enemies.

Acquiring adversaries and opposition is the unavoidable price of principle. Speaking the truth will earn a man enemies: it is a matter of *when*, not *if*, and the louder one speaks, the quicker the adversaries will gather. After all, a man cannot stand and genuflect at once: how can he stand up for truth if he's always bending the knee at the altar of taboo, observing popular pieties?

Palliating any and all imaginable parties offended, the man of appeasement has no religion. He is a loveless and a heartless creature. Do not befriend him. In his compulsive need to please all sides—the good and the wicked simultaneously—he is incapable of your friendship. The only true loyalty between human beings arises from a mutual, virtuous commitment to the truth. And the man unwilling to have enemies cannot, by definition, commit himself to the truth. Thus, an alternative expression of the same rule reads: *a man without actual enemies can have no true friends.*

Jesus said that "if the world hates you, keep in mind that it hated me first." While he stated this caution conditionally, he meant it as a guarantee: Christians can neither accommodate nor be accommodated by the world. Simply put, unless the worldly culture hates us, then we are failing at our job. Being God's spies does not mean that we hide our credo—in certain times, we mute the source of it. But we never mute the credo itself; the credo is what earns the righteous their enemies.

There exist only three types of friendship, two of which are mere shades of the single true form: true friends, friends of pleasure, and friends of utility. Friendships of utility are the most "accidental" form of friendship, according to the Aristotelian tradition, because the benefits they confer are material and wholly impersonal: in this case, you play with the kid down the block just because he has a swimming pool (even if you dislike him). Friendships of pleasure qualify as closer to true friendships because such friends are mutually attracted to something personal in one another, not a mere material benefit; however, the desideratum which mutually attracts friends of pleasure is not virtue. Only the true sort of friends are mutually attracted by one another's virtue, "like iron sharpening iron," as St. Paul writes.

Retrogrades, take heart! Audacious, intrepid men live and breathe who are worthy of your friendship, provided simply that you make *yourself* worthy of *theirs*! True friendships, as opposed to friendships of utility and pleasure, prove to be rare—but not non-existent. How does one find such men but by flying the banner and the colors of the retrograde. Signal who you are and what you stand for: the truth! You act in the name of St. Michael: you will do your utmost, until your dying breath, to give aid to the righteous and to vanquish the wicked. Fellow retrogrades in your area will recognize and join you if you're doing your job well.

Rule 12

Radicals form coalitions but retrogrades form fellowships.

A Coalition is a group of persons who are working together for a common intermediate purpose but who are simultaneously working in solitary capacities for divergent (and sometimes even diametrically opposed) final purposes. Coalitions ape authentic human fraternity, but, in reality, they tend to absolutize the individual, reducing peer coalition members to mere tools to be used in achieving a desired cause.[15] Once peer coalition members have served their purpose in achieving the intermediate cause, they may be discarded, and even reviled, as their usefulness has deteriorated. The dynamic between the demons in hell is akin to a coalition. Each fiend has only one true priority: himself; yet, he bands together with and uses his fellow reprobates to achieve his intermediate purpose: rebellion against God. If it were possible for

---

[15]   When people cooperate solely for the purpose of achieving a joint end, and not on the basis of love for God and one another, they belittle human dignity by treating each other as means rather than ends. Since God willed man's existence for the sake of man himself, it is improper to ever treat a person as a mere means: he must always be treated as an end, or else we run afoul of the divine will.

the demons to overthrow God, and if they achieved such arch-sacrilege, they would immediately set about quarreling with each other as they pursued their individuated goals.

A fellowship, on the other hand, is a group of persons cooperating for a mutual final purpose. Fellowships represent an authentic and salutary form of human fraternity, magnifying the human spirit and encouraging men to recognize the common destiny of the human race. Members of fellowships don't *use each other* to achieve a purpose; instead, they cooperate in a spirit of charity, viewing the good of their peers as an end in and of itself, alongside their final goal. The dynamic between the angels in heaven is reminiscent of a fellowship: the angels are united to one another in confraternity and service, owing to their common purpose, the glorification of God almighty. Since each angel wills, in addition to God's glory, the good of his fellows, even if it were possible for God to cease to be, and if God did in fact cease to be, each angel would continue to live in harmony with the other members of the heavenly host. So, while both coalitions and fellowships are species of focused special interest groups, they are as different as night and day. To be sure, the distinction between coalitions and fellowships is more than purely pedantic; it has real-world import of which the retrograde must be aware.

Radicals have no moral qualms about cobbling together coalitions of men who will today be coworkers but will tomorrow be enemies. For radicals, any means may be used to achieve an end deemed worthy or desirable. For radicals, even people themselves may be used as means. In practice, this means that a radical can work together with an opposing party (perhaps even a virtual enemy) if it helps bring about a desired result in the short-term.[16] Hence, in the radical worldview, the homosexual activist and the fundamentalist Muslim can associate in a coalition dedicated to defeating their common enemy, Christendom. It matters not to the homosexual or the Muslim, for the time being, that the homosexual believes that the Muslim is repressed by archaic fideism and that the Muslim believes the homosexual should be subject to the lash for his flamboyance. It matters not to the homosexual that the Muslim has in mind the terminal purpose of creating a worldwide caliphate. It matters not to the Muslim that the homosexual activist has in mind the terminal purpose of creating a worldwide regime of hedonism and licentiousness. These ephemeral allies are able to make use of each other and aid each other—despite their natural opposition—in bringing about a mutually-desired interme-

---

[16]   Note, on a pragmatic level, that modern history is replete with cautionary examples for why such a course of action should be avoided. After partnering with the Soviet Union to defeat the Axis in World War II, America had to immediately pivot to fighting fraught proxy wars against its previously allied coalition member. After partnering with Osama Bin Laden to defeat the Soviets in Cold War era Afghanistan, America had to crush an Al Qaeda organization that it had personally armed and sponsored.

diate goal on the way to divergent final goals. The radical camp is full of coalitions: anarchists and statists, feminists and Muslims, nation-states and illegal immigrants, trans-rights activists and women's rights activists. All of these groups are naturally antonymic, yet all are cooperating to swing the culture leftward. Once they have defeated their common ideological enemies, they will battle each other for supremacy, like the communists fought with the Nazis for control of the left in post-World War I Germany.

However, coalitions are anathema to the retrograde. The retrograde knows that he can do no evil so that good may come of it, that ends never justify means. The retrograde does not want to help, even accidentally, even far in the future, others achieve goals that are dissonant with his own ideology, which he considers sacrosanct. Instead, he wants to band together with like-minded men so that, in a true spirit of solidarity, they can intertwine their lives and honor in service of a common ideal, in service of those things which are transcendental, objective, and eternal: truth, goodness, and beauty. There's something treacherous and hateful to the man of good will to one day fight alongside a man that on the next day he will oppose. Further, as rooted as the retrograde is in Christianity, he knows that men are never to be viewed as means to an end, but only as ends in and of themselves. He, therefore, desires not to make use of other men but to serve alongside them, sharing conviviality, mirth, sorrow, joy, and the full range of human affect, *en route* to final communion.

Beyond these abstractions, there is a simple and gritty fact that the retrograde should take time to digest: in the long-run, coalitions don't work. While fellowships are, by nature, relational, coalitions are mechanical. Coalitions are prone to factiousness and infighting, since maintaining order and cohesion in a body made up of a motley assortment of ideological actors with deviating interests is an exercise in futility. True friendships are grounded in a pair's mutual love of truth and virtue. In a coalition setting, where most have disparate understandings of truth and misapprehensions of virtue, authentic friendship will be scarce and morale will suffer for it. It is axiomatic that a chain is only as strong as its weakest link. The links of a chain forged without friendship are brittle and rupture readily. So, since coalitions aren't predicated on authentic friendships, they can only be effective in the short term, till they collapse in cannibalism. Like Master Yoda says of the Dark Side when Luke Skywalker asks if it's more powerful than the Light: "No, no, no. Quicker, easier, more seductive." Although coalitions can quickly be assembled, since it's easy to find a group of men who share at least one interest in common, they're in constant danger of civil war. Since fellowships are predicated on friendship and ideological harmony, they're more difficult to form, in that it takes time to locate a group of substantially like-minded men, but they have staying power and indomitable strength. On the pragmatic level, eschewing coalitions is a short-term sacrifice for long-term success.

Retrogrades must demand ideological purity and uniform commitment to virtue in their ranks. It's the ultimate poison pill to increase our numbers while compromising our resolve. Commit to building fellowships with quality men; vigorously discriminate against wolves in sheep's clothing. We will ultimately win the day by presenting a united front girded with holy fraternity and steadfast resolve. Only then, in full bloom, will we be equipped to overpower coalitions of radicals, which are like mad dogs that bite indiscriminately.

Rule 13

There are four classes of ideologue, but only the first two constitute terminal worldviews. The retrograde must know them and be able to spot them in real time.

All adults of sound mind—yes, technically even radicals qualify—fit into one of the following ideological categories: **retrogrades** and **radicals** sit on the two opposite poles (sadly for now, the latter is a much more capacious group than the former). Between them are two kinds of moderate: **militant mods** are usually lukewarm liberals with some extrinsic reason for not calling themselves such, or for militantly clinging to a false middle; **mod-cons** are fainthearted but goodhearted people who sometimes call themselves "conservatives"—sometimes not—comprising the more or less decent folk who simply need good leadership but almost always lack it.

The emphasis of this rule is upon *public* engagement in dialogue.

Private engagement is a different animal altogether. As Dostoevsky often wrote, one-on-one engagement (even with a radical) proffers a unique opportunity at conversion, a rare gift from God. Together "getting into a jam," and out of it—or sharing some unexpected, solemn experience with no one else around—often makes die-hard friends out of bitter foes. Chance run-ins with estranged family members often lead to resolution; strangers on an airplane sometimes bond deeply after an in-flight near-miss; autograph-seekers dream about getting caught in an elevator with their heroes. These instances are some of life's most random and unexpected beauties. Capitalize on these opportunities, should they ever arise. But accordingly, they remain rare and unplannable.

Mostly, the retrograde will engage radicals, militant mods, and mod-cons out·in view of others. Moreover, the engagement will usually involve a public appeal, a one-size-fits-all address to any and all listeners. We will proceed with the simplest first.

In terms of public engagement, radicals always must be beaten at their own game—badly, definitively, and mercilessly. Publicly defeating them is the only conceivable way to reach them—and even then they almost never heed defeat's wisdom. Direct engagement in the combat of ideas fails for radicals, since their ideas fail facially, which is why they interrupt, shout, and set things on fire when they "dialogue" with retrogrades. By using these rules to overcome the radical's histrionics and tantrums, one sees they can quite easily be beaten but only very rarely converted (save for in private engagement, which again is rare). As such, usually public engagement with radicals doesn't accrue to the radical's benefit but rather for that of nearby third parties.

Those nearby third parties will always be either militant mods or mod-cons. Your target convert is the mod-con, who is open-minded, friendly, and usually center-right with a sinking suspicion about the truth. He is the unbrainwashed man of common sense. Militant mods, remember, are usually cowardly liberals who feel precluded by lifestyle accoutrements from self-billing as lefties, meaning they've made up their minds and already hate you almost as much as radicals do. Occasionally, you'll meet a militant mod who is truly militant about centrism rather than crypto-leftism. These are also non-convertible, but for different reasons.

The key to winning over mod-cons in your public forensics against radicals (or against cheeky militant mods, who sometimes like to argue for centrism) is to rhetorically obliterate your interlocutor and to *ooze* magnanimity in victory. By this, Aristotelian magnanimity is designated—not false humility. This means calm confidence in victory, without any regret, but with a thoughtful mien showing you've been victor many times before (i.e., this isn't new) and you'll maintain an element of mystery (i.e., surprisingly, you wish the best for your opponent: conversion). Usually, mod-cons will approach you privately after the debate, expressing their admiration, which will burgeon further if you look like a good-willed champ who's used to winning but is mysteriously somewhat aloof to it all.

In the dining car of a train traveling from LA to Chicago, on the way to a philosophy conference, I once debated a stately Chicagoan who declared to the blue-haired SJW next to him that the American dream was "a sham." I pointed out, with a friendly smile, that his *statement* was the sham: at least three of the four of us (my wife was next to me) were non-aristocrats eating good food and availed of comfortable means of travel, sitting together peaceably expressing conflicting ideas as the sun set over the beautiful Rocky Mountains in the distance. That *is* the American dream, I told him, explaining that he was defining the term "American dream" wrong (i.e., it's not a guarantee that everyone will be equally or fantastically wealthy). An hour-long debate ensued. I prevailed. The next day, I was approached by a mod-con who had been sitting two tables away and who described himself as a closeted-conservative Hollywood screenwriter— one who had been inspired by my performance to emerge from his cover. These fights are clearly worth having.

Rule 14

Any militant mod of this season will become an open radical in the next.

The development of a militant mod into a radical is merely a question of when, not if. That is, militant mods are typically radicals in training. They're waiting for something. The primary denizen of this class is either the "left-of-center Christian moderate" who has elevated his politics above his religion or the milder mannered secularist who identifies quietly left-of-center without explaining *how* left-of-center. Either way, the militant mod is a coward.

Think of it this way, why would *any* honest person strike a middle ground on an issue like abortion, for example? As always, abortion proves the rule. As has been pointed out so many times before, abortion either maliciously destroys an innocent life or it does not: the principle of the excluded middle won't apply here. There are no possible shades of gray on this issue. Yet a militant mod often operates, works, or socializes in conservative-ish territory, whereupon open association with the pro-abortion cause would create no small amount of personal inconvenience—the *bette noire* of both militant mods and mod-cons.

Accordingly, the militant mod refuses to cede an inch to strong anti-abortion argumentation while simultaneously abstaining from "owning" the opposite position. He's forced into an idiotic "no man's land" for which he resents not the radical but the retrograde (whom he already views as his enemy, secretly).

Think of a third-down-and-long situation in football: the offense knows it cannot score from the current field position, or even gain a first down, but still does not want to lose yardage before punting on the following down. In fact, the offense will be twice as determined not to lose yardage. Imagine militant mods waiting wistfully for their opportunity to embrace openly their leftism: they'll never cede ground because in their dawdling, they already feel sufficiently disloyal to their fellow lefties. Insecure, they refuse to lose any additional yardage in the meantime. They make for surprisingly staunch debaters, one of the many paradoxes of militant mods.

One of the best "tells" of a militant mod from a true mod is the object of their resentment: the latter retains an open mind and won't turn unilaterally bitter against retrogrades. *Conversely, the resentful, cowardly militant mod always blames the retrograde and never the radical.* It's both a categorical rule of the universe and a reliable tell.

There is at least one more sort of militant mod, however: the *actual* centrist. Whereas the mark of the first sort is his cowardice, the mark of this sort is his relativism. Whereas the first group makes relativistic claims *rhetorically*—regarding his own claims incred- ulously—some militant mods actually believe that both sides of the debate can be right at the same time. These are the militant mods who are true believers in centrism. Logic may not be on their side—these are the dupes of the "dictatorship of relativism"—but honest belief seems to be. As such, they won't blame retrogrades as aggressively as the first sort of militant mods. But militant mods they still prove to be: the belief in logical impossibilities embattles their intellect and will, eventually turning it against the retrograde. Proceed very carefully.

Rule 15

There is no room for optimists in the retrograde camp.

Optimism is voluntary self-deception. It's for this reason that Mark Twain once barbed, "The man who is a pessimist before 48 knows too much; if he is an optimist after it, he knows too little." Times are presently so dire—the fate of the West so truly hangs in the balance—that to survey our predicament with anything less than brutal candor is suicide. Necessity is so often the impetus for reform that if retrogrades are to have any chance of re-forging the culture as a true Christian republic, militant optimism about the state of society will have to be jettisoned. Optimism mollifies and reassures; however, one would have to be borderline schizophrenic to assess the present cultural milieu and come away reassured.

In the past half-century, we've witnessed, among other things, the universalization of abortion, the redefinition of marriage to include perverse sodomitical unions, the proliferation of drag-queen story hours (for children) at public libraries, the pornografication of movies, television, and music, a mass exodus of mothers of minor-age children out of the home and into the workplace, a divorce rate that has spiked to over 50 percent, an out-of-wedlock birthrate that has spiked to 40 percent, a trend towards legalization of euthanasia, a steadily declining birthrate, a pop-culture that extols drug-use and fornication, the metastasization of the welfare state, the dawn of the age of bi-weekly mass shootings, the steady expansion of the powers of the federal government, the heyday of the regulatory bureaucracy, and the decline of the practice of Christianity. What is there to be optimistic about? Absolutely nothing. The man of acumen should be aghast.

The medicine for our age is realism, nothing less. The retrograde must soberly survey the landscape, taking note of past losses and future vulnerabilities. Only then will he be able to begin addressing the crises hovering like albatrosses over the tempest-tossed seas of Western culture. Mod-cons have all but succeeded in painting contrived optimism as a requirement for the moral man. It's a way to cast their cowardly refusal to fight necessary battles as a virtue rather than a vice. Don't be fooled. Optimism is every bit as much an offense against truth as pessimism; it just happens to be better tolerated because it's couched in upbeat diction and because it's mistaken for charity by people of low intelligence. See the world as it is instead of how you want it to be, and you can make it as it ought to be; see the world how you want it to be instead of how it is, and it will remain how it shouldn't be.

Rule 16

Never utter, think, or imply that the retrograde merely upholds the status quo.

He does not. As every American should know, the retrograde is and must be capable of revolutionary action, whenever civil society and the common good depend upon it. History abounds with the colorful narrative of the righteous actions of such audacious retrogrades. Once per year, the celebration of the Declaration of Independence reminds us of a handful of such examples. Think of heroes such as Patrick Henry, Thomas Jefferson, and John Adams.

Conversely, radicals have portrayed—and gullible right-centrists have bought—the notion that a conservative must, by virtue of being *one who conserves*, always oppose decisive political action. This is a dangerous fallacy. Many have fallen for it. Yet, like Nietzsche wrote of the essence of music, the retrograde spirit must be half-revolutionary (Dionysian) and half-establishmentarian (Apollonian).[17] The first part invokes that wherever despotism shows its ugly face, dauntless men sever ties with tyrannical

---

[17]   Friedrich Nietzsche, *The Birth of Tragedy.*

old regimes; the second part requires that those same bold men—retrogrades to be sure—construct a just, stable, lasting regime upon the same principles over which the prior regime was abrogated.

In fact, the concept of a well-made republic requires it to *perdure*: it must be capable of stasis (Apollonian) in its foundational principles of justice and liberty while able to undergo small adjustments (Dionysian) in times of need. If the republic's foundational principles are deemed so broken as to be necessarily cast aside, then the need for a full-on change of regime will present itself. Imagine the debility when a republic operates on the faulty assumption that, categorically speaking, its people ought to be impotent to all occasions of necessary counteraction. No doubt, the radicals have been instrumental in popularizing this spurious, anti-republican worldview.

In other words, the Dionysian component of republicanism sustains the critical, chaotic, energetic spirit of the retrograde which activates whenever conditions have grown decadent, complacent, immoral, or tyrannical. On the other hand, the Apollonian component maintains, as long as possible, the ordered, traditional, stable spirit of republicanism operating within the abiding norms of law and culture (for as long as they can truly be said to survive). The retrograde credo does not invoke the latter only, but both together! As long as a republic stays true to its righteous foundational principles, stasis remains the watchword; when it strays from such principles, daring men must work drastic change through either revision or revolution.

Here's how it all plays out in real terms. Each year in America, the Fourth of July presents a ripe opportunity for meaningful explication of the principle of retrograde dualism: Dionysus and Apollo together. Moderate conservatives who began giving purchase to the "don't rock the boat" principle cannot even begin to account for salutary revolutions like that of 1776. The signing of the Declaration of Independence must be quite the enigma to such tepid celebrants of the holiday. At present, they cannot make heads or tails of it.

Yet they must be informed! The retrograde himself must tell the guests at his July Fourth barbecue what bad citizens they are, in their passivity; he must chasten them that they cut a perfect image of Jefferson's "timid men [who] prefer the calm of despotism to the tempestuous seas of liberty." That is, they cannot make necessary remedial changes, based upon natural law, to the republic as it groans under the tip of the savage spear of anti-Christian culture and beneath the weight of the despotic regime. At the Fourth of July, we Americans celebrate a right of rebellion inhering in God's nature. This right of self-defense requires retrogrades to be fully conscious of the Dionysian component of their own credo.

Rule 17

Never, ever "frag" a fellow retrograde.

This is a modification of President Reagan's rule: "Never say anything negative about a fellow conservative." The only misbehavior worth correcting a retrograde over is "selling out" by directly pandering to the enemy (and/or committing intrinsically evil violations of the Decalogue). The retrograde must never presume to impugn a fellow retrograde for his manners or style. Never correct a retrograde for a moderate or minor etiquette breach—especially if the retrograde being impugned has a strong track record of good work exposing radicals and cooperating with fellow retrogrades.

The most prominent current instance of the violation of this rule involves petty virtue-signaling by "white knight" retrogrades (along with a generous helping of *true mods*) who have appointed themselves the "tone of voice police." Not only does constant tone-of-voice self-recrimination by retrogrades condemn many of our best people and generate endless in-fighting, but most importantly, it promotes a right-wing version of a toxic ingredient of radicalism: relativism.

As the name implies, relativism absolutizes the relative and relativizes the absolute. Tone of voice is an article of each human being's *prudential judgment*, meaning that—harsh or mellow, sweet or sour, loud or quiet—it cannot be judged according to the same absolute moral and logical standards that one's words can be. Radicals prefer to police their interlocutors' tone of voice *precisely because* so doing allows them to obviate the plain truth by swapping what is absolute (text) for what is relative (tone). Radicals also prefer it because they fear the fact that righteous men often harbor heated righteous anger in view of radical injustice; radicals can avoid just chastisement by asserting that there is no proper occasion for indignation, which is a lie.

The retrograde cannot allow himself, or his righteous anger, to appear to be bested by the tepid illogic of radicalism. The foolish chastisement and finger-wagging at retrogrades by fellow retrogrades threatens to do just this, however. Accordingly, a retrograde should never get preachy or become a "white knight" with regard to another retrograde's angry tone of voice. Naturally, the radicals rejoice in such defeatism, fatalism, and infighting by retrogrades, since it wins for them a contest they could not otherwise win.

Reasonable minds *will* differ; to say reasonable minds *can* differ is to commit oneself to a certain eventual misunderstanding. No two human beings are possessed of a single, identical mind. Accordingly, it is only a matter of time before the finest two (theoretical) retrograde minds will come to disagree about some minor matter. Even middling matters of intra-Christian disagreement are not hills on which any of the good guys should die. We want them all to live to fight another day.

In this age, the good guys should err on the side of feistiness and fustiness with foes; they should err on the side of friendliness and fellow-feeling with friends. It's that simple. Yet the average Christian today is thrice as likely to cry out, "charity, charity," when he hears his fellow Christian dialoguing with the enemy. And he's thrice as likely to call down the thunder upon that grouchy Christian who might have darkened his tone of voice in dialogue with that anti-Christian. This rule enjoins retrogrades to reverse this perverse trend!

Lastly, one wonders: how should disagreement among retrogrades be handled? The answer is simple: charitably, professionally, technically, scholastically! Above all, privately! A retrograde's technical or logical errors of reasoning—never to be confused with a non-preferred tone of voice or "approach"—should indeed be pointed out by his friends. But the manner of correction should be private and dignified. It should be an amicable boon to the errant retrograde himself, with the purpose of restoring his *recto ratio*—right reason—a recovery he will, as a wise man, welcome. *Correct a sagacious man and he will thank you for it*, as the saying goes. Naturally, this sort of self-quarantine in the retrograde camp is to be lauded, not condemned. We reserve our condemnations for the radicals themselves, and for petty, turncoating infighting.

Rule 18

Circle the wagons around fellow retrogrades; come readily to their defense when they're in trouble.

This rule is the obverse of the exhortation to never frag a fellow retrograde. Yet, it deserves its own space on our list. While refraining from doing something negative is one thing, it's quite another to actively strive to do something positive. Affirmatively defending retrograde compatriots is necessary if we are to prevent our cause from being damaged by personnel attrition at the hands of radicals. It's worth remembering that radicals selectively target the most effective and intimidating retrogrades for political hit jobs and character assassinations. They assail those whom they fear most. As such, we must have a robust system of defense in place; we must cultivate a NATO-esque "an attack on one is an attack on all" mindset, a seamless entente. We must insulate each other from the smear tactics and yellow journalism so characteristically wielded by radicals. We're too few to lightly abide casualties.

What does circling the wagons look like in practice? When allegations about the misconduct of a fellow retrograde are being bandied about, go to the accused directly and solicit his side of the story, his defense. If his defense, taken on its own, is adequately plausible, extend to him the benefit of the doubt, believe him, and steadfastly advocate his story before the court of public opinion if the opportunity presents itself. If no opportunity to step forward in defense of an ally manifests, then a dignified silence is acceptable, since it does no harm and still carries with it an assumption of solidarity with one's fellows. If one has no direct or conversational knowledge about the pending allegations of misconduct but is confronted with questions about the situation, then he ought to take the defensive talking points that he has heard second-hand, and using common-sense and inductive reasoning, apply them the best he can, given his limited knowledge. Where right reason allows, the retrograde must fix his will on believing allies and disbelieving enemies. All things equal, the word of a retrograde should vastly outweigh the word of a radical. We know that the man who is trustworthy in small things is also trustworthy in larger things. It stands to reason that the word of a pro-life, pro-marriage Christian man is to be believed over a godless pagan radical.

It should be noted at the outset that there are exceptions to this rule. Unlike the radical, the retrograde knows he is bound by the eternal moral law and by the dictates of a well-informed conscience. He cannot blindly defend the illicit acts of his peers simply on the basis of political expediency—such a notion should be shunned by the man of high character. As

such, when a preponderance of evidence suggests
that a fellow retrograde has, indeed, committed *grave*
transgressions involving moral turpitude or *feloni-
ous* breaches of criminal law, then it is appropriate
to quietly withdraw one's support for the embattled
retrograde or to even discretely counsel him to take
leave of the public eye, repent of his misdeeds, and, if
applicable, resign his position of public trust. Unless
the disgraced retrograde has given rise to a public
scandal, there is no moral impetus to rebuke him
publicly. Quite the opposite, when it is necessary to
rebuke our allies, we should strive to rebuke them
privately, away from the voyeurism and prying of the
media. Do not give radicals further ammunition that
they can detonate on the retrograde cause. Where
only venial and superficial transgressions have been
charged to a fellow retrograde, we should dedicate
our communication to pointing out the absurdity of
wasting time and resources hyper-scrutinizing trifles.

We must also pause here for a scholium: just
because we ascertain that a retrograde ally is guilty
of misconduct does not mean that we must blindly
accept the sanction or redress that radicals suggest
for his punishment. Just because a man stands rightly
accused doesn't mean he stands rightly sentenced.
Nor is it a marker of lack of humility for a wrongdoer
to admit his guilt but quibble with an undue or overly
harsh chastisement. In order to maximize their political gain from the mistakes of their opponents, radicals
will always press for the most draconian measures to

be imposed on an errant retrograde. It is here that fellow retrogrades must instantiate the perfect nexus between justice and prudence. While allowing for, and even welcoming the application of just punishment to a wrongdoer, retrogrades must never allow their shame and embarrassment to turn them into a kangaroo court that rubber stamps even the most inapt and overly-harsh punitive measures. In our haste to uphold law and order, we shouldn't allow ourselves to begin prescribing the death penalty for parking violations.

It is in the realm of the application of justice that mod-cons falter to the highest degree; this is also where radicals make the most hay. Too often, in the wake of a scandal, mod-cons are overly anxious for their political party to be out of the spotlight and to have the news cycle pivot to less humiliating fare. As such, they accept, without a fight, the unduly harsh penalties proposed by radicals more interested in making a winning political play than in seeing justice borne out. This human-sacrifice, this friendly-fire, must be recognized and resisted.

Additionally, due to a nasty streak of superciliousness endemic to mod-cons, it's not uncommon for them to openly criticize (read: frag) allies after a transgression has occurred. This sort of opportunistic virtue-signaling is to be avoided at all costs. It's as if naïve mod-cons think that they will earn the respect of radicals by appearing sufficiently just to mete out chastisement to members of their own tribe. Clownish establishmentarians like Mitt "Pierre Delecto" Romney are genuinely shocked when they are calumniated by radicals when political circumstances so necessitate (e.g., in Romney's failed 2012 presidential campaign against Obama, then-Senator Harry Reid slanderously accused him of not having paid taxes for ten years), despite making a career out of finger-wagging at retrogrades in his own political party to the delight of progressives. Don't fall into this trap. Radicals will not hold the traitorous mod-con in higher regard than the rest of his ilk; instead, they'll happily accept the services of the useful idiot, and then discard him when he has naught left to offer.

Radicals, on the other hand, excel at rushing to the aid of a fellow radical in distress. They do it mechanically, automatically, without hesitating. Radicals never turned on Hillary Clinton, even in the shadow of scandals like Benghazi, Uranium One, and her e-mail server debacle. Instead, they supported her all the more vigorously. Radicals never called for President Obama's scalp despite his connections to scandals like "Operation Fast and Furious," the weaponization of the Internal Revenue Service against conservative organizations, and his Department of Justice's wiretapping of Associated Press journalists. They supported him all the more ardently. Radicals categorically refuse to cannibalize their allies. And retrogrades should take a leaf out of their book in this regard (subject to the exceptions set forth above).

Rule 19

The retrograde must loudly mock the general idiocy of the moral reasoning of the 1960s—especially "Boomer-isms" involving sexuality, courtship, and family planning.

Think of all the mortal dangers the radicals of that generation have normalized, popularized, and passed onto the next generation through the repetition of their harmless-sounding, yet fatal slogans: "college students should *live their lives* before they meet someone"; "before marriage, young people should travel and *experience the world*"; "young people should *learn by experience* what they like and dislike romantically."

In each of these, early and procreative marriage is clearly discouraged. Fertility is consistently handled as an inconvenience, at best. Each platitude sends the clear message that marriage and family will prove to be "a drag" and that life inheres in self-involvement and recreation rather than marital vocation.

Additionally vested within any given Boomer-ism, offset by a sort of weaponized ambiguity, there's always two components: a) some oblique reference to "experience" which somehow supposedly "contradicts" axiomatic moral reasoning (as if one has to try heroin in order to know that it is mortally perilous!); b) an encouragement toward sexual promiscuity or contraceptivity carried by the Boomer-ism's reference to experience.

In other words, Boomer-isms express an imagined inverse correlation between life experience and monogamy. These platitudes invariably stand for the proposition that sexual purity of all sorts is an admirable *ideal* (well . . . sort of) which doesn't usually work out for most people.

The retrograde's job inheres in highlighting, in private and public dialogue, that sex and procreation are indispensably linked in nature: whenever human beings have ventured away from the procreative Christian norms of sexuality—celibacy until the wedding day and chastity thereafter—catastrophe has devastated the population. In other words, the retrograde must deliver the message that sexual purity is not only for "religious people." It is for all people interested in living a happy, fulfilling life.

Not to mention, such Boomer-isms strongly work in the direction of the sociological phenomenon called "arrested development" (addressed further in the following rule), whereby a childish man is not presumed to come of age until he reaches his thirties or even his forties. Purveyors of Boomer-isms obsessively remind their offspring and grandchildren that they will not tender to them any moral advice. And they'll do so just before or after tendering to their offspring or grandchildren the above bad moral advice.

They make these specious claims on the ground that the younger generation must "live their own lives" and "find out for themselves," which is a performed, oxymoronic way of solidifying the bad advice they just gave.

The retrograde must announce loudly that the sun has risen and set on this anti-virtue-signaling by the ironically-titled Baby Boomer generation. Truly, history will know them as the generation by and for the radical culture-of-death lobby, which manipulated statecraft, warcraft, and even witchcraft (not to mention the globalist popular culture) to turn young, fertile couples against their procreative vocation. The Baby Boom generation represented, historically speaking, the terminal end of a widespread culture of life throughout all of human history (until roughly 1970).

Upon becoming parents to young adults in the 1990s and early 2000s, the Boomers—liberals, moderates, and "conservatives" alike—customarily instructed their offspring with the deadly advice not to marry and procreate until the middling years of adulthood wherein fertility rates have plummeted (see the next rule). Their justification for this advice usually involved acquisitive lifestyle accoutrements and existential-sounding platitudes like "finding out who you really are" or "finding your freedom" before "being tied down" to another person.

Now, not all Boomers are radicals, of course. But all of them lived and watched impotently amid the dispiriting, radical 1960s takeover of Western civilization. Accordingly, there seems to be near-ubiquitous generational psychic-scarring from living under such a repressive, subversive regime—the Boomer-isms of which have by now outlived many of the Boomers themselves, lasting over two generations. Even amongst non-radical members of the generation, Boomer-isms have produced a widespread generational ethos matching the tone of the militant moderates described above. Even many "conservative" Boomers—though not all—usually subscribe to the above experientialist, existentialist, libertine platitudes when it comes to dating or family planning.

The retrograde can overcome these mortal toxins simply by announcing to his elder relatives that he is "going in a different direction," which after all, they ought to well understand! There are countless hippie songs about just such a thing.

Rule 20

All retrograde youth (opting against the religious life) must be raised so as to be disposed to marry as young as possible and to procreate abundantly.

Retrogrades should consider this the "biological solution" to widespread political and moral problems: radicals are constitutionally sterile and can easily be beaten demographically by the provision of an abundant new retrograde generation in fifteen or twenty years. Simply put, we outbreed the radicals.

Today's ubiquity of sterility-promoting, radical Boomer-isms embodies the moral decadence presently popular in society. The preponderance of today's culture-of-death, wait-until-your-thirties philosophy regarding "family planning" has yielded small, materialistic families with manufactured, unnatural expectations regarding the amount of wealth required to "begin a family." The radical worldview has brainwashed virtually all of society that each and every responsibly birthed newborn requires his own pre-appointed bedroom, cellular data plan, college fund, and career path; without these already in place before baby's arrival, radical Boomer-isms instruct us, mother and father are just "breeding like rabbits."

On the contrary, parents of large families well understand that kids *love* sharing bedrooms; smart phone ownership and "screen time" *destroy* kids' imaginations and attention spans; college and career should be mapped not in infancy or elementary school but rather according to the established merits of middle and high school students. In other words, a man's career and wealth can afford to mature gradually, as his family does. Poverty (not to be confused with destitution) and thrifty living is good for a love-struck married couple fresh out of high school or college. There is plenty of time for their bank account to develop organically as their family grows: a single newborn baby or two proves remarkably cheap to care for.

The radicals, of course, are up against the facts of nature. The likelihood of infertility has almost tripled[18] if a couple waits to conceive until thirty years of age (compared against the same couple's rate at twenty years of age). Science does not lie. The human body's peak fertility occurs at twenty years old for a biological reason—bear in mind, this is the average age of a college sophomore. If only humanity were to return to non-manufactured, non-contrived, natural family planning by heeding the anatomical-physiological science on this matter, then young men and women would certainly rise to the occasion.

---

[18]   https://www.babycenter.com/0_chart-the-effect-of-age-on-fertility_6155.bc.

Imagine how different a culture of twenty-year-old first-time parents would look from a culture of thirty-year-old first-timers! Such widespread cultural expectations would be *prospective* in the sense that teens would customarily make radically different choices in anticipation of "real adulthood" beginning a decade prior to its present, presumed starting point. Arrested development, with its "perpetual teenage-hood," would be stopped in its tracks. Retrogrades have been mostly blind to the fact that an aggressive approach to the "bio solution" is a guaranteed path to eventual victory over the radicals.

Apart from the opportune statecraft implied by the retrograde "bio solution," the benefits which accrue to the young marrieds are plenary. When the sacrament of marriage is practiced properly and timely, men avoid the near-certain fate of becoming offbeat, self-obsessed, and lecherous (which awaits perpetually single men as an eventuality); women avoid the terminus of extended female "singlehood," growing shrill, insecure, and officious as they age without a spouse. Women who wed young, virtuous men customarily avoid these vicious qualities of resentment, since they are not habitually looking down their noses upon perverted, morally base husbands, who formed lecherous habits in the twenties and thirties.

Conversely, when a couple marries young, the man and the woman grow up in the virtues together in the adventurous milieu of the benign financial poverty of youth. Fresh on their new journey, the young couple will form good lifelong habits together. Salutary marital habits of teamwork and "specialized labor" were designed by human biology and the human lifespan to be inculcated in the late teens or early twenties rather than in the late twenties or early thirties (by which time bad habits have already solidified). A fruit must be picked when it is ripe, not long before or after: human beings simply aren't open to begin marital teamwork when they get too old. After all, the law of opportunity cost dictates that couples who wait until the thirties to marry may only have so many kids—even if they envision having large families. Having a truly large family mandates an early start.

An early start, in turn, mandates purposeful courtship. To initiate courtship, young men should clearly, plainly, directly ask young women for one-on-one dates. The request should be clear, specifically romantic in orientation, and plainly committal. Dinner and a wholesome activity should be expressed as on offer. For their part, young women should clearly, plainly, and directly accept the invitation by young men they are interested in. Just as the offer should be unconditional, so should the young woman's acceptance be: young women should *not* request a "group hang out," a "pre-date" coffee or lunch, or any condition precedent to the date. These all constitute breaches of nature. (Like matrimony, the first date necessarily involves two and only two people, some calculated risk, unmitigated mutual interest, and mutual commitment.) If any of these mitigators appear necessary to the young woman, she should simply and politely decline the young man's invitation.

Courtship should last only as long—no longer—as the man reasonably requires in order to discern his compatibility with the woman, and then to tender to her a timely marriage proposal. Such a period of discernment should occupy a varying span of months in duration, *not years.* As with the first date, the young woman should not condition her proposal-acceptance or -denial. All her relatives (presumably influenced by Boomer-isms) will certainly admonish her that she hasn't known him long enough; as noted above, culture-of-death Boomer-isms now advise youth to date for the greater part of a decade! If, accordingly, she feels inclined to request more time, she should simply and graciously reject his proposal.

If this rule is followed meticulously, Western dating and marriage will begin to make sense again. A return to classical courtship and prompt marriage will restore the Christian dignity of intersex relations. More importantly still, it will restore sanity to the home and the state.

Rule 21

All this Boomer-ist moral abandonment by our cultural elders has produced the "Miyagi Complex," which must be negated: Western civilization struggles to fathom a single sagacious denizen of our own Western, Christian culture fit to give sound moral or spiritual advice.

The complex works like this: virtue is so rare in the West that, in order to make any sense to the young Western mind, the perceived model of excellence must be sufficiently abstract or foreign. A mentor of the Far East turns out to be the only plausible candidate befitting the requirements of this semi-traditional moral exemplar. We are talking, of course, about the *Karate Kid*'s Mr. Miyagi.

Bankrupt Western culture sees literal and figurative "Daniel-sans" everywhere, fatherless either *actually* (like Daniel-san himself) or *functionally* (like any kid whose dad fails to teach him what he needs to know). Society's "Cobra-Kai," or secular humanist culture, prey on these many Daniel-sans, being raised defenselessly by single mothers, who usually love them but neglect to teach them (because they are incapable) manly virtue, like fighting for honor or self-defense.

Now, there's nothing inherently problematic about the "Miyagi complex," except the abject lack of Western morality and leadership it reveals. Mr. Miyagi, after all, proved an excellent mentor to Daniel-san: he loved him better than most fathers of our day. But we cannot all be Daniels: Daniel was lucky enough to live in the same apartment complex as Miyagi. Most are not so lucky. Therefore, we must unlock the true virtue hibernating in the Christian breast and the Western canon. Only then will moral exemplars emerge in the West.

Once more, there exists undeniable logic in the Miyagi Complex: Mr. Miyagi was tough, wise, kind, and *involved*. By contrast, the fathers and grandfathers of most young men in the West no longer teach them to fight (defensively); they are pragmatic rather than wise; they prove self-interested rather than kind; and most of all, they remain *utterly uninvolved* in the moral lives of their young. Simply put, there are virtually no wise elders in our midst, meaning our generation must rise up and dare to live virtuous, faithful lives! That way, our own children can—like all human beings throughout history, except for the last two generations—look to its elders for the location of moral treasures, practical shortcuts, and avoidance of moral pitfalls. The tough part, of course, is doing this without real-life exemplars!

The Boomers attempted to hybridize Christianity with libertinism, which is like trying to draw a circular square. But the duplicitous aim of their attempt to "circle the square" has been quite persuasive, at least in the view of the popular culture. Let's examine this in light of some previous rules.

Christianity has been so sanitized in the popular mind that its teachings on chastity have fallen upon popular ears as utterly worthless and even silly. In this arena, as well, the Miyagi Complex looms large: if the message of true chastity somehow gets transmitted to a child of the West, it will always be through some Oriental means, most frequently through one of the martial arts. For example, "boxer's chastity"—think of the trainer Mick telling Rocky to "lay off the pet store dame" during training—will usually be welcomed, but never Christian chastity. In other words, the pseudo-chastity of the boxer is merely pragmatic, not moral.

Blame Boomer-isms, and the defanged version of Christianity they represent, for this toxic phenomenon. It is most unnatural for a society's moral exemplars to be abstract, removed from the young. Nature mandates that the young learn by immediate access to wise leaders *close at hand*. Somehow in this generation, we must triumph over the additional cross of a largely bankrupt generation of elders: the only conceivable way of recovery inheres in looking to the One True Man, Jesus Christ, and the saintly disciples he inspired over the course of two Christian millennia. We must become our own exemplars for the sake of our children.

Mr. Miyagi was a fine model of protective, virtuous manhood in the 1980s. *Karate Kid* was a timely film in the sense that it instructed the next generation after the Boomers, who desperately needed the message in whatever conduit they could find it. But it is high time for a new generation of retrogrades to live deliberately and morally—so that we may end what the Baby Boomers began. We must be the heroes and champions of our own families, for our own sons and daughters.

Rule 22

Do not ingest the poison pill of conventional wisdom.

General Patton once observed, "If everybody is thinking alike, then somebody isn't thinking." What has come to be viewed as safe and irrefutable wisdom—namely, that cache of platitudes uncritically imbibed by the Baby-Boomer generation in their own time and then mechanically regurgitated by them as sacred truth, a one-size-fits-all miracle balm for all situations—is really a roadmap for how to be outfoxed by radicals and lose the culture in just a few short years. As sanctimonious as the Boomers have been in doling out their empty bromides, the critically thinking retrograde must be equally diligent in rejecting them.

Why the Boomers are comfortable scolding retrogrades for not closely adhering to their losing set of rules of engagement is anyone's guess. Consider this: in just a couple of decades, from the 1960s to the 1970s, America's culture was successfully coopted and transformed by a loud minority of strung out radicals while "conservative" Boomers, hamstrung by their ill-conceived sensibilities, offered mere token

resistance, giving way at every turn. Twenty years'
time gave us no-fault divorce, abortion on demand,
ubiquitous contraception, mainstream feminism, the
working mother, religious indifferentism, the welfare
state (in the form of the Great Society), draconian
environmentalism, destigmatized drug-use and fornication, and a watershed federal piece of gun-control
legislation (the Gun Control Act of 1968). Yet, conservative Boomers feign indignance when younger generations refuse to march in lock-step with their feckless
advice. It's like the Cleveland Browns demanding—
with straight faces—that the rest of the NFL's teams
should make use of their playbook. No thanks; we'll
look elsewhere, anywhere else. Boomers, you failed
us; your time is up. Kindly retire to the ignominy of
the shadows and rid us of your bad ideas once and
for all.

So what are examples of the sorts of Boomer-isms
that are to be spurned with extreme prejudice? The
list is long, but it's worth producing some notable
examples for posterity. Boomers are obsessed with
cosmetics over substance: they insist on scolding retrogrades for the "tone" that we use when doing ideological battle against radicals. They have made "thou
shalt be nice" into the eleventh commandment. They
are constantly finger-wagging at zealous young retrogrades who proclaim truth with fiery speech. They
insist that retrogrades must use a sanitized speaking
style devoid of passion, devoid of flair, devoid of any
hint of righteous anger about the iniquity of the left.

They believe that it's inherently sinful to use speech with teeth, to show ire, and to meet evil ideas with harsh rebuke, when, in fact, Thomas Aquinas teaches just the opposite (it's disordered *to not act on righteous anger, to let evil go undenounced*, according to the Angelic Doctor).

Bold, clear, and sometimes angry speech is the only kind of speech that is effective in calling the *hoi polloi* out of the stupor into which they've been placed by the constant deluge of radical propaganda. If Trump's 2016 presidential campaign shows us anything, it shows just how foolish the mindless Boomer attachment to anodyne speech really is. We were breathlessly told by conventional pundits during the course of the election that Trump would have to soften his tone to win the general election because "suburban women don't like negativity." In the wake of Trump's resounding victory, have the talking heads recanted their flawed advice? Have they reconsidered their attachment to insipid, idle affirmation? Of course not. *Nevertheless, what matters is what you say, not how you say it*; don't let anyone tell you differently. The biblical prophets and the apostles were caustic at times in delivering the good news, when the occasion called for it, when the actions of their flocks occasioned stern rebuke. Don't let pusillanimous Boomers convince you that there is an inherently sinful tone— there isn't. What matters is substance; style is prudential and individual. The mystical Body of Christ has many parts—some of us are called to be the killer-T cells. Perhaps, had the Boomers delivered more jeremiads in their own time, we would have been spared rampant societal cancers like abortion, feminism, and divorce.

Another self-evidently flawed Boomer-ism is that peaceability is inherently virtuous, that peace is an end in and of itself. Cowards never admit their cowardice—they always cloak it in the extravagant garb of magnanimity. When Boomers have sounded the call for retreat on a whole slew of pressing cultural and political ideas, they have always couched their decision to stop fighting "settled cultural battles" in a slavish commitment to national unity and peace. But as Christ himself tells us, peace isn't to be embraced at the expense of justice—it is for this reason that he announced that he came to bring not peace but a sword. Not only is it not virtuous to roll over and accept radical victories in regard to fundamental cultural questions such as the protection of life, the preservation of marriage, and the unchecked expansion of a runaway federal government, it's actually sinful. But Boomers have declared that their lack of fight on bellwether issues is actually noble. Don't be deceived. Fighting isn't inherently sinful. Sometimes it's sinful not to fight.

Perhaps the most noxious Boomer-ism, the one most stridently and priggishly espoused, is that it's inherently wrong to pronounce moral judgment on others. It has been said that an insufficient amount of Christianity is more dangerous than no Christianity at all. The campaign against "judging" others is proof of this. Sitting on their high horses, Boomers have ripped out of context and weaponized one of the few Bible verses that the lukewarm actually know, to the detriment of Christ and his Church, truth, and Western culture.

Where Christ exhorts "Judge not, that you be not judged," he's certainly not telling us to refrain from labeling certain agents and actions as "good" and others as "evil." If he were, then he couldn't, without contradicting himself, instruct us elsewhere to "Judge with right judgment" and "If your brother sins against you, rebuke him." What Christ is telling us is to not presume to *condemn* others, pronouncing definitive judgment on the eternal destination of their souls, since this is God's prerogative. He's also telling us not to harp on the relatively small flaws of others to the neglect of our own larger flaws. However, the righteous man, whose flaws are relatively benign compared with the vices of baser men, actually has a duty to correct others. This is why the Church has long recognized that "admonishing the sinner" is one of the spiritual works of mercy. Not only should we not refrain from making moral judgments about others, we are actually bound in our consciences to make such judgments in order to guide the culture in a just direction and to care for the souls of our fellow men. One must affirmatively distinguish what is good from what is evil in order to know what to do and what not to do, to know what to vote for and what not to vote for, to know when to celebrate and when to fight, and to know who is good and who is bad. To deliberately abstain from making moral judgments about agents and actions is to embrace moral relativism (the arch-heresy of heresies), the denial of objective truth itself.

While it is impossible to, here, compile a plenary list of the various and sundry false platitudes that together constitute the platform of "conventional wisdom," one should be guided by the rule "common sense is not so common." Whatever advice is rendered to the retrograde, he must take pains to examine it critically before heeding it. No "rule" is to be considered beyond reproach, save those reflecting the eternal moral law. We must, therefore, be inquisitive of the track record of every dispensary of advice. If he is reciting the playbook of an unsuccessful era, we must be firm and loud in our rejection of his ideas. To draw from an axiom that *is* based in truth, it is insanity to do the same thing over and over again while expecting a different result. If we do not allow ourselves to be quagmired by sacrosanct tropes from the past, we have a better chance of winning back the culture of the future. Think critically and stay sharp. Never be content to be part of the herd.

Rule 23

The memory of the Western public is exceedingly short, pathetically undisciplined, and never to be feared.

Mod-cons have been deeply conditioned to dread future political reprisals anytime they dare to contemplate substantial political action that threatens to drag the culture rightwards. So fearful are the mod-cons—especially those empty suits holding elective office in legislative bodies—of potential backlash at the ballot box in the event that they act too decisively in bringing to fruition a conservative policy, that they succumb to what's fairly characterized as political paralysis. The reason for this phenomenon is simple: when weighty conservative policy initiatives (the ones that radicals really fear) are being floated and debated, a uniformly hostile and unapologetically perfidious media springs into action: focus groups filled with disgruntled constituents are spotlighted, rigged polls are conducted, fringe demonstrations are televised, and the airwaves are flooded with talking heads shouting vitriol. The punditry begins a seemingly endless series of broadcasts dedicated to underscoring an alleged wave of populist, grassroots resistance welling up in response to the conservative initiative. It's made to seem as if the mod-con and his legislative compatriots are entirely isolated in the ideological sea, as if the public mood is such that voters can think of nothing other than the next election, wherein they can race to the ballot box and gift the mod-con's job to his political rival. Don't be fooled.

In spite of the chest-puffing and manipulative antics of a disgustingly biased media, the ballot-box retribution that we're told is looming right around the corner is nothing but a specter, a chimera devised by radicals to stymie retrograde progress by stealing the already-scant courage of our wishy-washy representatives. The Western public is anything but a disciplined, principled, intellectual voting bloc. The average voter is embarrassingly ignorant about current affairs, and his political memory is slightly shorter than the average news cycle and slightly longer than a goldfish's. Some alarming poll numbers bear out this sad state of affairs. It turns out that only 36 percent of Americans are able to identify all three branches of government; in fact, 35 percent can't name any of them. A whopping 60 percent of Americans are unable to name the political party that controls the House of Representatives and the Senate. In the run-up to the last presidential election, more than 40 percent of Americans could not name the Republican or Democrat vice presidential candidate. Twelve percent of Americans don't even know who the current vice president is! Clearly, a nation of political wonks we are not.

Data paints a similarly dismal picture of the public's ability to harbor stable, cogent political sentiments over any significant periods of time. Consider this: around the time of the passage of the Affordable Care Act (i.e., Obamacare), 59 percent of Americans opposed the law (many did so vehemently), in contrast with just 39 percent who favored it. So unpopular was the bill that in the aftermath of its being codified into law by the Democrats along a straight party-line vote, Republicans gained, in the 2010 midterm elections, a staggering sixty-three seats in the House of Representatives (putting them back in the congressional majority) and six seats in the Senate, including one seat in Massachusetts, which they had not won since 1972. Mind you, the eponymously-dubbed Obamacare was *the signature legislative achievement* of Barack Obama's first presidential term, and, in retrospect, perhaps the crown jewel of his entire presidency. Yet, despite the legitimate, non-fabricated grassroots public disdain for Obamacare circa 2010 and the unbridled popular animosity for its authors, just two years later, in the 2012 presidential election, Obama spanked Mitt Romney, earning 51.1 percent of the popular vote and 332 electoral college votes in contradistinction to Romney's 47.2 percent and 206 electoral college votes.

Public sentiment shifts with regard to the war in Iraq also testify to the fickleness and forgetfulness of the American voter. In March of 2003, still reeling from the 9/11 terror attacks, an overwhelming majority—72 percent—of the American public favored the invasion of Iraq. Only a few years later, that number had dropped off drastically, with 61 percent of Americans *actively disapproving* of the war. Seeing as how the circumstances surrounding the beginning of the war had remained in relative stasis in the intervening years, it's difficult to explicate such an abrupt about-face except by recourse to voter attention deficit disorder.

Then there's the infamous case of Anthony Weiner— or as many affectionately call him, "Carlos Danger." Weiner served in the House of Representatives from 1999 to 2011, till it came to light that he, then married, had sent lewd photographs of himself to a female college student. As a result of the scandal and in the face of a congressional ethics investigation, Weiner was forced to resign from the House of Representatives. Not one to be deterred from the siren song of a cushy political career, a short time later, in May 2013, Weiner announced his candidacy for mayor of New York City (a political gambit that the *New York Post* unforgettably captioned "Weiner's Second Coming"). By late June 2013, the freshly disgraced former congressman, whose crotch-shot had recently broken the internet, had *surged to frontrunner status in the mayoral race by a comfortable margin of five percentage points*. If it were not for the fact that new allegations of Weiner sexting with additional women surfaced shortly thereafter, he might have actually, in phoenix-like fashion, rejuvenated his political career with a tenure in Gracie Mansion.

The point of the foregoing anecdotes is to drive home one theme: voters have tragically short

memories, memories which would rival those of clinical amnesiacs. How constituents will react to news of
an elected official's advocacy for a particular issue or
involvement with a given initiative should be the last
thing perturbing the mind of said official. Members
of the Western public are detached to a fault from
the political cosmos; they're irresponsibly indifferent, preferring to indulge in fatuous, smut television
like *Game of Thrones* and the *Masked Singer* rather
than to pay adequate attention to their most basic
civic responsibilities. It's nothing short of madness to
imagine that the same folks who can't identify the
current majority party in the United States Senate or
name the secretary of state will be intently following
their elected officials' stances on nuanced policy controversies one-and-a-half years out from the nearest
midterm election in hopes of ferreting out points of
disagreement. As it is now, elected officials can essentially engage in any political errand—even to the point
of scandal—with impunity, so long as they make nice
and tickle the ears of their constituents with splendid promises of government candy in the two months
leading up to an election. Given the advanced state
of decay of the West, it's a laughable proposition that
voters are going to hold elected officials accountable
for any articulable reason, much less for a perfectly
defensible, if perhaps "unorthodox," position.

Nevertheless, in the realm of American politics,
the Republican Party consistently allows radicals to
hinder the pace of its legislative agenda by heeding media attack-dogs' manufactured warnings of

impending ballot-box apocalypse ("blue-waves" and such) if Republicans move forward in implementing conservative policies. Even in the aftermath of Donald Trump's election, when Republicans controlled the executive, legislative, and judicial branches of the federal government, the Republican sellouts failed to make good on any of their major legislative promises: they didn't defund Planned Parenthood; they didn't repeal or replace Obamacare; they didn't stanch the flow of illegal aliens pouring into our country. And the primary reason for their failure to act and secure these victories was fear of voter retribution—fear of losing their power and majorities. Due to their baseless fear, cowardly Republicans squandered this generation's best chance at making significant strides towards a more just and conservative America. The bitter irony is this: despite two years' worth of legislative impotence from Republicans (from 2016–2018), they *still* lost the House of Representatives in the 2018 midterm elections.

The message is clear: to any retrograde political actors, forge ahead in your endeavors. Do not fear the phantom menace of voter backlash two years out. It's a sheer invention of a media class that is trying to interdict your progress, the archetypical tempest in a teapot. Put first things first and second things second and you'll get both.

Rule 24

When a rival or overlord like Alexander the Great comes to visit you, offering gifts, be the philosopher Diogenes the Cynic! Tell the radical mob or despot that you want nothing from them except that they "stand out of your light."

In a rule above, the retrograde exemplar was Alexander; in this case, the exemplar is his adversary Diogenes, who scornfully rebuffed the great ruler. Consider Plutarch's account of the strange encounter between two of the most dissimilar great men in history:

> Thereupon many statesmen and philosophers came to Alexander with their congratulations, and he expected that Diogenes of Sinope also, who was tarrying in Corinth, would do likewise. But since that philosopher took not the slightest notice of Alexander, and continued to enjoy his leisure in the suburb Craneion, Alexander went in person to see him; and he found him lying in the sun. Diogenes raised himself up a little when he saw so many people coming towards him, and fixed his eyes upon Alexander. And when that monarch addressed him with greetings,

and asked if he wanted anything, "Yes," said
Diogenes, "stand a little out of my sun." It is
said that Alexander was so struck by this, and
admired so much the haughtiness and grandeur
of the man who had nothing but scorn for him,
that he said to his followers, who were laughing and jesting about the philosopher as they
went away, "But truly, if I were not Alexander,
I wish I were Diogenes." and Diogenes replied
"If I wasn't Diogenes, I would be wishing to be
Diogenes too."[19]

Here's the moral of the story: never accept a gift or
a nicety from an opponent, much less from the "social
justice" mob. Never embrace an entitlement—bread
or circuses—offered by Machiavellian politicians.
Bread and circuses prove to be the wage by which
radicals purchase their ill-gotten office and by which
the individual is parted from his liberty.

Acceptance of economic favors from radicals puts
one into their debt and robs the goodly man of his
honor and self-possession. In other words, be *magnanimous*, offering aid to all in your path, but accept-
ing it only from the most trusted friends—even then
only with great hesitation. Once in a great while, one
meets a radical not completely inoculated against the
winsome allure of extemporaneous Christian virtue.
Do not hold your breath, but you may just convert a
radical through your example of magnanimity.

---

[19]   Plutarch, *Alexander*, 14.

Aristotle defines the virtue of magnanimity in the following terms, "The great-souled [magnanimous] man is fond of conferring benefits, but ashamed to receive them, because the former is a mark of superiority and the latter of inferiority."[20] He continues, down the page, "It is also characteristic of the great-souled man never to ask help from others, or only with reluctance, but to render aid willingly; and to be haughty towards men of position and fortune, but courteous towards those of moderate station, because it is difficult and distinguished to be superior to the great, but easy to outdo the lowly . . . it is like putting forth one's strength against the weak."[21] In these short lines, Aristotle explains why the magnanimous Diogenes would rebuff a man so admirable as Alexander: because he alone was worthy of a challenge. He alone was worthy of Diogenes's haughtiness.

The retrograde must reclaim classical magnanimity for himself and for his people. He must learn to emulate both the great-souled man's virtue and his contempt for the mob. Aristotle closes by mocking pretenders to magnanimity who merely "imitate the great-souled man, without being really like him, only copying him in what they can, reproducing his contempt for others but not his virtuous conduct. For the great-souled man is justified in despising [vicious]

---

20   Aristotle, *Nicomachean Ethics*, IV, 3, 24.
21   Ibid., IV, 3, 26.

people—his estimates are correct; but most proud men have no good ground for their pride."[22]

Retrogrades, be restored to magnanimity, reclaiming righteous contempt for vicious men; but first, reclaim virtue! Remain unattached and unindebted to the mob.

---

[22]   Ibid., IV, 3, 21–22.

Rule 25

The root of cultural decay is feminism: end feminism to end radicalism.

The family is the building block of society. It is the wellspring and training ground of future generations. It is the natural setting where the virtues are learned: piety, morality, prudence, frugality, decency, etiquette, and every good thing for our youth. As the family goes, so goes society. It is precisely for this reason that the family has found itself under full-fledged radical assault in the past half-century. If radicals succeed in rending asunder the family, in reeducating our kids, they will have won the culture. This is why Vladimir Lenin boasted, "Give me just one generation of youth, and I'll transform the whole world."

The primary vehicle that radicals have used to undermine the family is feminism. It is a bald-faced lie that the purpose of feminism is to achieve "equal rights" for women. That's merely the party line fed to the ignorant and the bitter. The animating purpose for feminism has always been the overthrow of the "patriarchy," the headship of men in society and, particularly, in the family. It is a little-known fact that, even as far back as the 1848 Seneca Falls Convention (the coming-out party for "first-wave" feminism), the attendant bluestockings declared, "The history of mankind is a history of repeated injuries and usurpation on the part of man toward woman, having in direct object the establishment of an absolute tyranny over her," and that, "In the covenant of marriage, [the wife] is compelled to promise obedience to her husband, he becoming, to all intents and purposes, her master." Empowering women legally and politically is, for feminists, but a mere means to end patriarchy.[23] Once the rightful leaders of the family, fathers, are deposed, radicals know that they will be free to remake the family into an arm of their apparatus, or at the very least to dismantle it as a bastion of the old order. Like Maleficent from *Sleeping Beauty*, radicals fear nothing as much as the righteous, broad-shouldered man.

However, patriarchy will not lightly be cast off. It has been willed by God from the beginning of creation. This is the reason why Adam had authority over Eve (as evidenced by him naming her), even prior to the Fall, in the state of original justice. It's why God empowered Abraham, Noah, Moses, Aaron, and Joseph to guide his people. It's why Christ selected twelve men to be the princes of his Church. It's why there continues to be, as a matter of Christian doctrine, an all-male priesthood. It's the reason why, throughout human history, "There is not, nor has

---

23   Estelle B. Freedman, *No Turning Back: The History of Feminism and the Future of Women* (New York: Ballantine, 2002), 17.

there ever been, any society that even remotely failed to associate authority and leadership in suprafamilial areas with the male."[24] A rebellion against patriarchy is a rebellion against God himself—it's a rebellion against the order and intelligibility of the universe. As with other failed systems like Marxism, when man attempts to set aside human nature, the consequences are dire.

For years, feminists have been attempting to subvert marriage and family life in an attempt to disrupt patriarchy. They have tasted a great deal of success in their endeavor. No-fault divorce has become the law of the land, yielding a marital attrition rate of about 50 percent. Abortion, which "frees" women from maternal duties, is legal and rampant, producing fifty-seven million human casualties in the United States alone since 1973. Contraception, another insulator against the chief gift of marriage, children, is virtually ubiquitous, with 98 percent of sexually active women having used a contraceptive method at some point. Feminists have also taken to attacking motherhood, shaming housewives for being "lazy" and "unambitious" and pressuring them to take up needless glamor-careers for the sake of "empowerment." Currently, 70 percent of women have abandoned minor-age children in exchange for careers outside the home, delegating mothering duties to disinterested nannies and sterile

---

[24]   Steven Goldberg, *Why Men Rule: A Theory of Male Dominance* (Chicago: Open Court, 1993), 15.

day-care centers. As Pope Pius XII once lamented, when the mother is absent from the home, it becomes "desolate for lack of care," with members "working separately at different hours in different parts of the city and hardly ever meeting one another, not even for the principal meal or for the rest at the end of the day's work, much less for family prayers." Even in many otherwise-functional, traditional marriages, the wife (contrary to scripture—e.g., Titus 2:5, 1 Peter 3:1–7—and reason) has usurped her husband's authority and headship over the family, resulting in a *de facto* leadership vacuum. Hen-pecked, uxorious men are now the rule.

The foregoing feminist machinations have produced wages of the most fetid sort. The culture has quickly become crass and despondent. Drug-addiction, pornography, violence, and crudity abound. Mass-shootings, which are almost always perpetrated by young men from broken homes, are now routine. Of a recent sample of fifty-six school shooters, a scant ten were raised in a home with both biological parents.[25] Studies show that "a father's absence increases antisocial behavior, such as aggression, rule-breaking, delinquency and illegal drug use—especially among boys."[26] Since 1999, the general suicide rate has

---

[25]   Bradford Richardson, "Link Between Mass Shooters, Absent Fathers Ignored by Anti-gun Activists," *The Washington Times*, March 27, 2018, https://www.washingtontimes.com/news/2018/mar/27/mass-shooters-absent-fathers-link-ignored-anti-gun/.

[26]   John C. Goodman, "Are Liberals at Fault for the Breakup of the

increased by 33 percent in the United States. However, the female suicide rate has increased by 53 percent to the male's 26 percent. For people between the ages of ten and twenty-four years old, the suicide rate increased by 56 percent in the ten-year span between 2007 and 2017. What's more, kids raised in a single-parent home are more than twice as likely to commit suicide as their peers raised in traditional homes.[27] Even without poring over facts and figures, one can palpably sense that we're living in a time of general Western malaise—an unseen specter has long haunted us, sending a frisson down the spine of society.

Feminism has failed to deliver even on its empty promises to women. In their paper "The Paradox of Declining Female Happiness," economists Betsey Stevenson and Justin Wolfers analyzed women's happiness trends between 1970 and 2005. To the surprise of many, they discovered that despite women's newfound "liberation" and "progress," female contentment scores decreased every decade from the time the survey was administered. In other words, despite a spate of new legal rights and protections, women are less happy than they were in the "dark days"

Family?" *Forbes*, March 16, 2015, https://www.forbes.com/sites/johngoodman/2015/03/16/are-liberals-at-fault-for-the-breakup-of-the-family/#229fc1a027ec.

[27]   Sid Kirchheimer, "Absent Parent Doubles Child Suicide Risk," WebMD, January 23, 2003, https://www.webmd.com/baby/news/20030123/absent-parent-doubles-child-suicide-risk#1.

of widespread housewifery. In 1960, women's self-reported happiness was greater than that of men. By 2005, men were the happier sex. It's clear that we've been sold a defective product.

Central as it is to the health of the culture at large, the family simply cannot be overlooked as the primary locus of the battle for the soul of society. Thus, if the retrograde is to rescue society from the clutches of radicals, he will have to do so by purifying and reinvigorating the family, the most noble and ancient of institutions. This necessitates that we discredit and decisively reject the saccharine hemlock of feminism and its contumacious rebellion against patriarchy. Men, rise up and grasp firmly the mantle of leadership in your homes. Insisting on wielding your God-given scepter of authority isn't bullying—it's your sacred duty. Hold fast to your wedding vows; love your wives; teach your kids diligently; but flee from any temptation to cede your rightful authority, giving way to a practical matriarchy. If we diligently attend to our families, providing for them, educating them, loving them, guiding them, and *growing them*, in one generation we will have taken back control of the culture from the deviants who have long plotted its demise.

Rule 26

The retrograde must use Saul Alinsky's shrewdest, trickiest rules for radicals against the radicals themselves.

We will examine how to specifically reverse two of his rules: 4 and 13. Respectively, these two rules read: "Make the enemy live up to his own book of rules"; "Pick the target, freeze it, personalize it, and polarize it."

First, let's "polarize" Alinsky's rule 4: "Make the enemy live up to his own book of rules." Alinsky admits openly that he was inspired, naturally or supernaturally, by the tactics of the Devil, who simply cherishes the concept of hypocrisy. According to both Scripture and Tradition, Lucifer was and is fascinated by both the *concept* and the *implementation* of hypocrisy, employing it wherever opportune on his own behalf and pointing it out in others whenever expedient (which, of course, indicates his implementation of a sort of meta-hypocrisy, a "hypocrisy within hypocrisy").

No surprise, then, that Alinsky's favorite tactic involved decrying hypocrisy and anything else *looking like* hypocrisy in his political opponents. Every American general election cycle, radicals across the land furiously forage the political landscape for any and all indicia of the slightest instance of hypocrisy by the "religious right," which they find, of course, since all humans make mistakes. What's truly diabolic in this *modus operandi* is the startling consequence that Americans have generally given purchase to the radical lie that an act of hypocrisy by Party A equates to an automatic "score" for his rival, Party B. Naturally, this consequence of unintelligent voter behavior continues to incentivize radicals to weaponize hypocrisy.

We must turn the tide by making *radicals* meet muster, a double-twist to be sure. In other words, force the enemy to live up to his own rules about enemies living up to their own rules! In order to accomplish this, Christians must become more adept at weaponizing the radical concept of equality: *radical impunity against Christians—in the name of equality—violates justice.* Retrogrades must resolve this abuse of so-called equality for themselves.

For example, consider the radical community-organizing effort from 2012 until 2017 that resulted in the temporary coercion of Christian bakers in Colorado to produce cakes for celebrants of homosexual civil unions (until the Court of Appeals holding was overturned in the Supreme Court in 2018 in favor of the bakeries.)[28] Supposedly "value-neutral" jurisprudence in America (such as the decidedly anti-Christian

---

[28]   *Masterpiece Cakeshop v. Colorado Civil Rights Commission*, 584 U.S. _ (2018).

holding by the Court of Appeals) has *never* actually been neutral, notwithstanding its claims. Without other options, the retrograde must negate the enemy's legal tactics culturally. He must do this by showing that—one way or another—an immoral application of one of the "rules for radicals" against a Christian can easily be weaponized by that same Christian.

In the absence of an eventual overturn by the Supreme Court, Christian bakers might have ironically employed Alinsky's rule 4 by posting signs in their bakeries saying: "All profits from wedding cakes for homosexual civil unions will be diverted exclusively to heteronormative religious causes." This would classify as a defensive tactic, as it rebuffs prospectively against enforceable requests by homosexuals for wedding cakes. Sure enough, between 2012 and 2017, Christian cake shops might have been legally required to violate their Christian scruples; but this way, at least they could use the profits to strike against the very occasion of the radicals' oppression. More importantly, their signs would likely have deterred homosexuals from requesting (i.e., requiring) them to provide such cakes. The radical insistence on a certain type of equality under the law would, in that case, work in favor of Christians, for once! The Christian baker would have successfully reversed Alinsky's rule 4, even in the face of legal defeat.

Alinsky's rule 13—being offensive rather than defensive—allows for a more aggressive response to the same circumstances: "Pick the target, freeze it, personalize it, and polarize it." Operating on the basis of rule 13 (from 2012 until 2017) the retrograde might have struck back, locating and then patronizing bakeries run by radical, anti-Christian homosexuals and forcibly requesting Christian- and heteronormative-themed wedding cakes. This would be the retrograde's more ambitious way of affirming the exclusivity of man-woman marriages. Pick the target (i.e., an opposition bakery), personalize the message, and polarize what they attempted to do to Christians. The radical left won't "live and let live." So why should we? Forceable viewpoint discrimination in the realm of baker-harassment "cuts both ways," after all. The retrograde must see to it that it does. While the Supreme Court eventually rendered the issue moot in 2018, the "hot button" issue of Christian bakeries and homosexual wedding cakes provided an excellent opportunity to exercise the retrograde's moral imagination. It will prove both necessary and worthwhile to anticipate what retrogrades may do—defensively and offensively—in a foreseeable day to come when the ultimate holding may not be as innocuous to Christians as that rendered by *Masterpiece Cakeshop v. Colorado Civil Rights Commission (2018)*.

In practice, abiding this rule of Alinsky's (13) serves to cross-reference the rule for retrogrades enjoining a perennial offensive counterattack. The reader can plainly see how much more effective the offensive application of Alinsky's rules are than the defensive! Once more, always be on offense!

Rule 27

When it comes to the justification of our retrograde principles—especially public expressions thereof— let rules be rules and exceptions be exceptions.

Don't sweat the explanations for exceptions to rules! In public forensics, radicals will always pose to retrogrades weaponized hypotheticals which falsely insinuate self-contradiction in our worldview. Do not allow this cheap score. They do so on the Alinskyan basis of categorically "making the enemy live up to his own book of rules,"[29] since cunning Alinsky knew that very few rules of human life suffer zero exceptions. Almost every rule under the sun bends the knee to outliers or extenuating circumstances.

Alinsky also knew that right-wingers prefer to be thorough in their answers to questions. And yet even two or three honest seconds of responsive stammering or thoughtful re-formulation by today's retrograde can be used very effectively by radical opponents to cast the retrograde in a dubious light. So be prepared to give a boilerplate reply: "E.M.B.L." *Exception makes bad law*. Memorize this, practice saying it fluently,

---

[29]   Saul Alinsky, *Rules for Radicals*, Rule 4.

and take its meaning to heart. It will save your skin in public debates.

In order to "win" such debates, radicals—who have the unenviable charge of defending wrong ideas—must accordingly seize upon *any* means whatsoever of gaining the ostensible advantage and *any* opportunity to lend to retrogrades the appearance of self-contradiction. Because petulantly demanding a frangible explanation for some obscure hypothetical exception is very easy to do, it is one of the radical sophists' favorite instances of shadow play.

Early twentieth-century radical John Dewey may have been the first one to lead radicals down the path of seeking never-ending exceptions to rules, especially as a rhetorical device against historical conservatives (like Aristotle) of the Western tradition. Dewey posited that nature is not an assemblage of *kinds* of things:[30] he reasoned that human categories and stipulations about the world must all involve distinctions of *degree*, not *kind*. For Dewey, the difference between any two mammals and a reptile would be marked by a sliding scale of similarity, which for him exists in the only real sense in the human mind. After Dewey, relativism—the sheer will to overcome moral rules of nature through runaway subjectivism—did the rest of the work carrying radicals to their present position, from which they balk at all of Western civilization's hard moral distinctions.

---

[30]   John Dewey, *Logic: The Theory of Inquiry*.

Dewey's nominalism, together with relativism, provides fertile ground for radical demands about hypothetical exceptions. Retrogrades: never trip over such radical exception-mongering. Simply express that "exceptions make bad law" (E.M.B.L.) and move on. Style points can be added with some other small rhetorical nuances, but anything beyond stating "E.M.B.L." should be brief.

Sometimes, the retrograde will have to respond to *legitimate*, yet contrived, radical exceptions. For example, imagine being tasked with defending the general truism that because women are less fast and strong than men, they should not be allowed to play in the NFL. This should be an easy argument to win. But a radical debater would certainly advert to the undeniable yet stark fact that somewhere in the world a particular woman may be faster or stronger than a particular man. On this basis, a radical will petulantly demand: *so where does anyone get off saying "less fast and strong?"*

Many entertaining responses present themselves as candidates for the retrograde's rejoinder, but the upshot of his argument must at least include a reference to the comparative average speed and strength of men and women—and an accusation that (based upon it) the radical does not believe his own argument. After all, the rate of female injury and dejection in a hypothetical female-allowing NFL would be sky-high. Rules must be based upon averages not outliers.

Other times, the retrograde will confront utterly illegitimate exceptions, wherein the "exception" can be either wholly countenanced on its own and/or dispelled by recourse to the above means. Either path will suffice. For example, in abortion debates, radicals will never go long without adverting to their favorite argument for infanticide—that is, so-called rape and incest "exceptions." In this case, the retrograde can point out either that this is a false exception since murdering the offspring of a rapist or incestual remains murder or that the number of rape- and incest-inspired abortions are numerically negligible anyway. ("Tabling this minority of cases, do you then concur that all other instances of abortion—and maybe these as well—constitute murder?") Either response is suitable, but prudence and random history will require that a retrograde choose between them in "real time."

In general, the primary play in the playbook remains the utterance of "E.M.B.L." Don't be slow to use it. People know intuitively that it is correct, anyway. Saul Alinsky was counting on the strong tendency of right-wingers to wax philosophical in debate; make him pay for this error by dispensing with right-wing navel-gazing and casually retort with this pithy quip.

Rule 28

For radicals, the "issue" is never the real issue.

Don't be fooled, whatever it happens to be, radicals' talking point *du jour* is invariably a mere ruse aimed at achieving a darker, more nefarious, more strategic long-term goal. Mod-cons often make the mistake of engaging radicals on the substance of their talking-points, as if radicals are advocating for or against a given policy in good faith. But this is folly. The talking-points of radicals, their issues of the day, are always mere trojan horses for accomplishing a deeper agenda. When radicals take up the mantle of a given issue, it's as an avenue for pursuing something far more profound. So, you'll never be able to get a hardened radical to abandon his endorsement of, let's say, expansive firearms restrictions, even if you offer irrebuttable proof that crime rates are lower and murders are fewer in areas where legal gun carriage proliferates.[31] The issue, for the radical, was never truly an intolerable level of violent crimes; that was all a

---

[31] John R. Lott, Jr., "Guns, Crime, and Safety: Introduction," The Journal of Law & Economics 44, no. S2 (2001): 605, 610, doi:10.1086/341243.

decoy—a convenient setting for emotive lip-service aimed at providing the justification for a re-imagined society.

Mod-cons would be well-served to understand, for example, that the debate over gun-control isn't about reducing deaths; it's about making people more dependent on government by depriving them of self-sufficiency. Likewise, the debate over abortion isn't about "a woman's right to choose"; it's about "freeing" women from the home by enabling women's careerism. The debate over unfettered immigration isn't about relieving the world's poor, tired, huddled masses; it's about ushering in globalism and undermining the sovereignty of the nation-state. The debate over raising taxes isn't really about balancing the budget; it's about income redistribution. The debate over "climate change" isn't really about protecting the environment; it's about handicapping the economies of first-world nations so that third-world nations can achieve parity of wealth. The debate over gay-"marriage" isn't about "equality of rights"; it's about debasing and undermining Matrimony and the family, which are viewed as patriarchal and oppressive. The debate about "trans" rights isn't about respecting human dignity; it's about undermining the moral order and crushing sexual taboos. The "true believers," those wonks who become embroiled on the radical side of the foregoing fights, fail to comprehend that they are mere pawns in a larger game that is being played by cleverer people. If you don't know whether or not you're a pawn, then you're a pawn.

On a meta-level, what radicals are really pursuing is a humanist "utopia"—a world without borders, class distinction, sex distinction, and wealth inequality, a world where each man is free to live out his unique, "artistic" identity, doing as he pleases, unshackled from "arbitrary" constraints placed upon him by a "domineering" ruling class. It's a subjectivist-existentialist vision wherein each man can make of himself what he wills, serving not God, but his own whims and thereby, (ostensibly) the community. Till this ultimate stage of the radical vision is achieved, the state must be grown and empowered so that it can be used as a bludgeon to implement the unnatural policies that will ensure the attainment of the longed-for utopia. But, out of fear of backlash, radicals have to scheme to bring about their new order in secret. They can't broadcast what they plan to do, because it would prove fatally unpopular. So they have to implement their grand vision piecemeal, never tipping their hand, till all becomes clear in one chthonic denouement.

Be reminded that the radical vision is an inherently godless vision, one that must be heartily rebuffed by the retrograde. Efficient causes (creators) imbue their creations with final cause (with purpose). Since God is our creator, we cannot "choose our own purposes in life." To decide man's purpose is God's unique privilege, and he has decreed, once and for all, that our purpose is to know, love, and serve him. Living life outside of these parameters leads only to misery and ruination. That said, we need to attack the radical vision in its unmasked form. There is no use debating an endless litany of decoy issues with radicals, except to temporarily stave off an attack; rather, we need to attack the philosophical errors that are at the core of radicals' doctrine. Becoming bogged down in the morass of policy minutiae with radicals is a fool's errand, since their mania for the utopian state moves them to ignore the illogic of the many planks of their platform, just as the tail wags the dog.

Rule 29

Never let your judgment be rushed or altered because of an alleged "emergency"; all serious policy initiatives deserve thorough vetting.

Radicals love crises because every crisis provides them with leverage to fast-track their agenda under the cover of an exigency and its corollary hub-bub. As we've already alluded to, since truth and reason are on the side of the retrograde and not the radical, where there is robust and fair public discourse on a given subject, the soundness of the retrograde's position (and the unsoundness of the radical's) will be made manifest. A prime example of this is the national debate over the permissibility of abortion: in the decades since the Supreme Court handed down its foul decision in *Roe v. Wade*, public opinion on abortion has flipped, and America has transitioned from a predominantly pro-choice nation to a predominantly pro-life one. The ambitious radical, therefore, must advance his agenda through sleight of hand and gimmicks, seeing as how when he fights toe to toe with the retrograde, he is destined to lose. Guerilla warfare is the radical's wheelhouse by necessity.

Since a thorough discourse on a policy matter undermines the position of the radical, then it is intuitive that he should seek to expedite such discourse or circumvent it altogether. However, this poses a significant problem: even the most jejune political muggle is well-aware that weighty policy decisions should not be made in a hurry, as haste in important matters lends itself to cataclysmic mistakes. The radical must therefore proffer a reason sufficient to justify shortening the standard public-vetting period. Yet, a sufficient reason is difficult to manufacture—even for seasoned manipulators. The radical is clever though. He bides his time and waits, and the twenty-four-hour news cycle eventually bails him out, providing him with a much-needed catalyst—a headline sure to touch a raw emotional nerve with an overwrought public. Any story with a plausible nexus to a policy initiative that the radical wants to advance will do. Needing no more prompting, the radical and his media spin machine go to work, agitating for immediate action (in the form of the adoption of the radical's policy initiative, of course) to be taken to remedy the problem at the heart of the news story before any more lives are lost or damage is done (etc.).

Recent times are dogged by exemplars of the foregoing *modus operandi*. Each time a mass-shooting occurs, we are barraged by the same nauseatingly stale calls for "common sense gun legislation." Any time a tragedy befalls a group of immigrants crossing the southern border illegally, we can count on having to abide a torrent of lobbying for comprehensive immigration reform (i.e., amnesty). Every time there is particularly inclement weather, perhaps a spate of hurricanes, we know that calls for anti-climate-change legislation will climb to fever pitch (because hurricanes didn't take place before the industrial revolution). Every time that, due to a glitch in someone's insurance, they are denied funding for a serious operation, we know that calls for universal government health care are right around the corner. Even though these types of stories make the headlines for the very reason that the events they describe are particularly severe and relatively uncommon, radicals play-act that the reported goings-on are a daily bane for society and that, if decisive action isn't taken quickly, the results will be catastrophic and irreversible. For whatever reason, perhaps because of their insatiable thirst for popular adulation, mod-cons find this sort of feigned urgency difficult to ignore, especially when they feel the weight of their ill-informed but boisterous constituents' gazes. Channeling Chicken Little running around aimlessly squawking about how the sky is falling, panicking mod-cons rush to cooperate with radicals on new policy initiatives even before the sociology or science tasked with exploring the cause of the tragedy has been settled.

But this self-defeating impulse *must* be avoided. The principled man cannot allow himself to be held captive by his swirling, mercurial passions. While the dictates of the virtuous man's emotions will often overlap with the dictates of his reason (since Providence saw fit to gift the passions to man to move his will in harmony with the movement of his intellect), there is no guarantee of emotive infallibility east of Eden, even in those of most august and noble character. It's the intellect's purview to discover the truth with certainty; the passions' *raison d'etre* is to inflame man to love truth. And while the passions often light up in recognition of that which is right and bristle at that which is wrong, they remain a very fallible epistemological tool. It is evident then that correct policy decisions are the offspring of reason, not emotion. Owing to this, it is a trap to be avoided to rush to make policy decisions, bypassing thorough debate, in the weeks after a tragic event. Retrogrades must never act on passion to the neglect of reason; yet, when radicals piggyback advocacy for their policy initiatives on the heels of a recent tragedy, this is precisely what they're goading us to do. To be sure, national tragedies like Sandy Hook and the 2017 Las Vegas Shooting shocked and made heartsick every retrograde in America. Nevertheless, the retrograde knows that inaccurate policy "solutions" are two-headed serpents: they're dangerous affronts to liberty and simultaneously impotent for preventing recurrence of further tragedies of the same kind.

The risk of inflicting mortal wounds with ill-considered policy decisions will always be nearly infinitely greater than the risk posed by a reluctant, procedure-bound legislature. One need look no further than to the grand failed political experiments of the collectivist governments of the twentieth century for proof of this. The retrograde must be prepared to suffer slings and arrows for being "heartless" when in his methodical deliberation, he refuses to run blindly over a legislative cliff. Truly stoic leaders will always have to carry the cross that is to suffer the myopic bellyaching of their shortsighted flocks. It is far better to suffer such mortification than to act rashly, either in a fit of rudderless emotion or in an effort to showcase one's wealth of compassion. When we take action too hastily, abridging the salutary deliberative process so crucial to healthy self-governance, we are almost assured to err in our judgments, swallowing the poison pill of radical policy initiatives. Resist this at all costs.

Rule 30

The retrograde must be tough-fibered but chaste! Accordingly, his watchword should be "coarse but never crass." As will be understood below, he must have "thick skin and a weak stomach."

Unadorned language representing rugged, time-proven ideas—one of these being sexual purity—is one of the most desperately needed paradoxes in the defense of civil society. Tough, non-backpedaling, unapologetic language is one of the retrograde's handiest tools against the statecraft and psy-ops of the radicals. Here's why:

The radical's unsung, implied anthem, "thin skin, strong stomach," forms the perfect opposite to the retrograde's, and it provokes the strangest one-two punch imaginable. The radical scandalizes the young with brazen sexual lewdness that pulls further and ever further underwater the flagging morality of our culture. That part of the story is well told. But surprisingly frequently, the radical downshifts into "shrill prude" mode and churlishly wags his finger in the faces of the decent should they presume to use a plastic straw or a cigarette in his presence.

All human beings have an inbuilt drive for morality; radicals act "thin skinned" in order to virtue-signal their perverse, anti-Natural Law pseudo-morality, which is truly an anti-morality. Believe it or not, the profile of the American radical turns out to be one-half libertine eco-terrorist and one-half pearl-clutching parish councilwoman.

It's genuinely odd to find so much Puritanism remaining in American far-leftist ideology; it's still odder how no one seems to notice. "Thin skin, strong stomach" proves to be the strangest symptom of modern Western civilization's half-Puritan, half-Enlightenment schizophrenia. It is especially prominent in post-Protestant places like America and England. At the beginning of the modern era, the radical alchemist concocted a toxic bromide titrated with one very inert (Puritanism) and one very radioactive (Enlightenment) element: *these were the two elemental forces of Modernity.*

One minute, these people are showing school kids how to put a condom on a vegetable, and the next, they're lecturing you about the "dangers" of trying to leave the hospital without the newest model of car seat for your newborn. They're actually crazy. These creeps switch from obscene-gesturing school pervert to sighing, "tsking" schoolmarm with demoralizing swiftness. But there's a method to their psy-ops. In fact, it's almost genius in the bewilderment caused to the opponents of the radicals. Consider *Seinfeld's* Elaine Benes who, in one episode, chides a smoking pregnant mother: "You realize what that does to the *fetus*, don't you?" In a later episode, Elaine dumps her pro-life boyfriend on the sole basis of his impassioned defense of fetuses. Is this veritable schizophrenia? No! The viewer discovers, simply, that Elaine never cared about fetal health at all but only about the elimination of one of the pre-ordained radical *bette noires*: smoking.

Elaine's easily typified radical proposition reduces to the absurdity that it should be legal (and not at all discouraged) to intentionally slaughter fetuses but illegal (and aggressively discouraged) to engage the small to moderate risk that they be somewhat harmed by ingested smoke. Or, still more absurdly, Elaine has signaled to her boyfriend (and all *Seinfeld* viewers) that defending the *lungs* of fetuses is admirable but defending their *lives* is morally unacceptable. Welcome to Clown World.

Also, consider singer Katy Perry, who spearheads something she calls "purposeful pop,"[32] sometimes "woke pop," by posturing against gun violence, hate speech, and NFL racism. Anyone who hasn't seen her perform, or glanced at her lyrics, might mistake her for an officious, principled female social worker. However, she sings songs like the one called *Last Friday Night* which, by all appearances, was written to attract the attention of twelve-year-old girls. Indeed it was: the libertine re-education of America's youth through pop culture cannot come to pass unless they first pos-

---

[32]   Twitter, 2/9/17.

sess these youth as a captive audience. In the chorus of this bizarrely puerile-sounding sonic arrangement ("puerile" even for Katy Perry), the sometimes moralizing, finger-wagging schoolmarm upshifts back into school pervert, singing: "Last Friday night, we went streaking in the park, skinny dipping in the dark, then had a *menage a trois.*"

Bear in mind, this lyric falls in the *chorus* of the song, being loudly repeated several times. Radicals, moderates, and even apathetic conservatives allow their children to listen to that filth! To put this all into context, recall how radicals and even moderates will literally bemoan—complete with loud histrionics—the use of any modifier besides the newest neologism designating the mentally retarded, while in other venues the selfsame radicals and moderates will argue vehemently, in the name of human progress, to abort all fetuses pre-diagnosed as mentally retarded. They're wicked. The radical credo is the soul of insanity and self-contradiction: *thin skin, strong stomach* shows them for what they are.

Combat this by showing off your "thick skin and weak stomach." Remind the radicals that you will not amend your language to befit their neologistic statecraft, wherein they control thought by monitoring language. For instance, tell them, "I will not be shamed into using your new term for the mentally retarded; I will, however, always defend their right to life and, moreover, to live happily free of radical politics of de-personalization and eugenics."

Rule 31

Don't allow radicals to personalize the general.

When I was in graduate school, I served as a teaching assistant for an undergraduate moral theology class taught by a kind and erudite bishop. The good bishop was always brimming with interesting stories from his time in ministry, and one day, he related an experience that has always stuck with me, as it was particularly poignant. The bishop, striving to be a good shepherd in his diocese, had agreed to teach a lesson at a local Catholic secondary school. As part of his lesson, he was outlining the Church's teachings on life and the dignity of the human person. After he explained to the class the Church's teaching that in-vitro fertilization is morally illicit since it separates the unitive and procreative aspects of conjugality and reduces the body to a mere mechanism for procreation, he saw a girl's hand shoot up. The bishop called on the girl, expecting a good-faith question aimed at clarifying some point of doctrine that he had glossed over or had explained unsatisfactorily in his haste to deliver his lesson. What he got was a defiant gotcha challenge—one aimed at making him look harsh and judgmental. "My mom had me through in-vitro fertilization," the girl blustered. "Are you saying that I'm not as much a person as anyone else?"

Such is the method of radicals. Expect no decency from them. Since they cannot compete in the realm of abstract ideas and logic, radicals have adopted an aggressive method for putting retrograde interlocutors on the defensive: they manufacture an insult out of thin air by taking the general, impersonal concept being advocated by the retrograde and apply it to a sensitive real-world situation to make it seem as if the retrograde is attacking the *actor* or the result of the action (in the case of a child conceived through in-vitro fertilization) instead of the *action* itself. Retrogrades must be ready for this sort of cunning if they are to prevail in public dialogue and rally followers to their cause.

The radical's method of personalizing the general is effective for three reasons: first, it *distracts* the retrograde and the audience (if done in a public debate) from the retrograde's thread of thought; second, it *steals the initiative* from the retrograde, putting him on the defensive and making him feel as if he must reassure the radical that he bears him no personal animus; third, it *manipulates* the audience, making them feel sympathetic to the radical's untenable belief out of pity for his condition. Since the method of personalizing the general is so endemic in radical dialogue, we must learn to negate its efficacy. With but a little forethought, this is not a difficult thing to do.

One of the best ways to handle personalization of a topic is to simply depersonalize it, meeting the radicals +1 with our own -1, therefore arriving at a mean of zero, back where we began. If the retrograde argues, for example, that abortion is evil and is met with the standoffish rejoinder that the radical's mom "had an abortion; are you calling her evil?" the retrograde should simply pivot, saying something to the effect of, "I've never met your mother and she's totally irrelevant to this debate. Whether or not she's had an abortion has no bearing on whether murdering a baby in utero is evil, so let's stick to material points." By saying something to this effect, the retrograde points out the illogic of talking about the radical's mother during a policy debate. He also straightens the kink that the radical has attempted to throw into the otherwise straightforward subject matter by explicitly denouncing the attempt to hijack the conversation with irrelevant facts. By scolding the radical in this manner, the retrograde also subtly scolds every member of an audience who was tempted to be spun off by the radical's red herring. Further, by reasserting his point that abortion is evil in his rebuke of the radical's attempt to personalize the conversation, the retrograde organically places the debate back on track, recalling it to its original subject matter.

Another effective technique for subverting radicals' attempts to personalize a given topic is to couch assertions in higher authority. For example, when meeting the challenge, "my mother had an abortion;

are you calling her evil?" it is salutary to reply, "What I think is neither here nor there; what matters is what the Church teaches about abortion: that it's murder." Radicals are more circumspect to attack powerful collectives than they are to attack individuals. It would be politically disastrous to insult billions of Christians worldwide by publicly denigrating the Church. As such, by joining one's opinions to the doctrines of a powerful institution, the retrograde gives himself some measure of insulation from radical petulance. Also, if retrograde views are seen as "mainstream" in that they fall within the penumbra of a respected organization's beliefs, then people will be loath to label the retrograde as "cruel" and "judgmental," because in so doing, they'd be besmirching friends, family, and neighbors who may also be affiliated with the organization. Whatever method one chooses for circumventing radicals' attempts at personalizing, the central concept remains the same: we must learn to distinguish the condemnation of the sin from the condemnation of the sinner. We must learn to distinguish the attack on an idea from an attack on a person.

Whatever the retrograde does, *he must avoid seeming worried about looking "mean" or "uncaring"* in response to the radicals' attempt to take personal umbrage from a general idea. As spineless and unprincipled as they are, mod-cons habitually fall into this trap, and they never seem to learn to avoid it from the failures of the past. As soon as radicals see weakness and waffling in response to their personalization and crocodile-tears, they will press their perceived advantage *ad infinitum*. Sensing blood in the water and a fearful, disoriented prey, they will continue to ramp up their aggression till eventually they corner and devour it. Never be afraid to tell a radical how few hoots you give about a particular action done by his mother, one way or another. Once radicals know how unafraid you are of appearing "mean" and how indifferent you are to their sordid personal lives, they'll reverse course, opting for some other cheap trick to try and win the day.

Rule 32

The monolithic, private right-wing "boycott" of leftist companies is a sham; gutsier approaches to commercial confrontation are superior.

The primary party inconvenienced by badly organized boycotts is the boycotter himself. Moreover, the quiet refraining from patronizing a certain business is no political action at all: voluble publication of the boycott is a necessary component of increasing its efficacy and momentum. Personally, permanently refraining, for example, from patronizing Starbucks proves utterly futile because by definition there is no chance for the boycott to spread to likeminded individuals. On the other hand, boycotts are frequently quite effective if sizable, definite in time period, and well-coordinated. (But if monolithic, indefinite in duration, or non-orchestrated, they are virtually useless.)

Now, there is nothing immoral in inefficacy. Many right-wingers adopt household policies involving refraining from consuming Starbucks, for example, which is perfectly fine. We designate such households "monolithic boycotters." But such campaigns are simply ineffective and shouldn't be considered the standard for retrogrades, whose watchword is not only principle but also efficacy. More often than not, the monolithic boycotter proves to be the one virtue signaling to the retrograde, not the other way around. That is, the lone boycotter is usually the agent of hypocrisy, although it is a counterintuitive thought. Here's why.

Generalizing for a moment, the profile of this "too busy to get involved" right-winger is that of one who is usually trying to substitute his ineffective private boycott for recognizable, real political action against the wicked radical company (being taken by retrogrades). Still generalizing, the monolithic boycotter is usually the one on his high horse, rallying against the vastly more effective retrogrades who are actually making a dent (perhaps as they drink coffee). All this adds up to a hypocritical preachiness heard all too often from uninvolved conservatives.

Far more effective—if more laboriously orchestrated—techniques and actions against radical corporations are smear campaigns like old-fashioned picketing, aggressive contra articles or commercials, or celebrity interventions; for example, "Starbucks supports the following monstrous causes: [list them]." Damaging ads and published attacks frequently work because global companies prize their "brand"— which equates to future profits—as highly as they value current profits. When an uninvolved conservative monolithically boycotts, he damages neither the evil company's *present* profits (because billion-dollar companies don't notice the opportunity cost of a cup of coffee) nor its *future* profits (because the boycotter has done little or nothing to damage the company's brand). The company's evil continues unabated in the face of the monolithic boycott.

In the logic of the fight, damaging the radical company's priceless brand is the most effective thing a retrograde can do, even if (for the sake of argument) he's consuming the company's product as he does it. There is little or no contradiction in consuming coffee while attacking the coffee's wicked allocation of profits, because the retrograde never formally cooperates in Starbucks's intents.

The best attempt to bring down a radical brand is the direct attempt, either forcing a change in profit allocation or actively ruining the brand's reputation. Once more, the watchword is not just principle but *efficacious principle*. Making needed sacrifices is the most beautiful aspect of the fight; making needless sacrifices (like refraining from a leftist company's coffee) is one of the silliest. If one is going to fight drawn-out, arduous battles, one needs priorities!

Rule 33

Stop heralding unwelcome news of progressive victories by wishfully proclaiming (channeling Japan's Admiral Yamamoto circa Pearl Harbor Day) that radicals have "awakened a sleeping giant."

The platitude is beyond being banal and naïve; it's triumphalistic in the most tone-deaf way, and therefore, it must be anathema to the retrograde if we are to see our worldview win the day. Yet, in the face of shameless leftist mischief (the re-imagining of the American healthcare system through the Affordable Care Act, the attempted coup against Donald Trump by nefarious deep state actors, the attempt to usher in Catholic women priestesses in the Amazon Synod, etc.), we have heard *ad nauseam* that certainly the latest bits of news from the front will *finally* push passive observers over the edge, awakening in them a fighting spirit sufficient to spur them to rise up *en masse* and finally vanquish our ideological foes, restoring common sense and decency to the public arena. Horsefeathers. Countenance the fact that most men don't have fighting spirits (or at least have dulled them with lives of vice and indulgence), and of the few that do, most need their dormant fighting spirits to be invigorated by an even smaller strata of strong men with vision.

It is an illusion of the most dangerous sort to believe that, coming eye-to-eye with an injustice, men will naturally rise up and take the necessary actions to set the world aright again. The retrograde should constantly and soberly remind himself that the fallen human condition is such that feeble men, on the whole, will adapt to and even embrace even the most perverse and unpalatable regimes, so long as they have ample entertainment, cake, and carnal pleasures. Billions of people have endured, many with smiles, severe repression at the hands of tyrannical states like Red China, North Korea, the Union of Soviet Socialist Republics, and Germany's Third Reich. These regimes have denied people fundamental freedoms such as familial integrity, freedom of speech, and freedom of religion—strictures far beyond those fathomable to the fatted Western mind. And yet, despite the spartan conditions and dystopian laws of such states, political dissension was or is underwhelming, even moribund. Never underestimate man's ability to abide an evil to which he has become accustomed. The uninspired man eventually accepts his lot and resigns himself to suffering it rather than risking his few creature com-forts (and perhaps, even his life and liberty) in favor of justice, intangible as it is. (Only the unworldly and noble man can risk tangibles for ideals.) Like in the film *High Noon*, complacent men, who are, sadly, the vast majority of the race, will make every excuse to avoid the inconvenience and risk that accompanies the defiance that is part and parcel of being a retrograde. Thus, that sleeping giant so giddily touted by armchair-activists is often no more than a paper tiger.

Moreover, to many, the sleeping giant metaphor represents a groundless assurance that goodness will ultimately win the ongoing cultural and political wars, despite a seemingly endless succession of radical triumphs in battles, which forebode just the opposite. Hence, the metaphor is false catharsis, a dishonest emotional pacifier for those who need to self-soothe in the wake of bad news. It is a failure to come to terms with objective reality. Such a failure to grasp the current state of the world is a roadblock for the retrograde agenda. In order to fight the wiles and schemes of radicals, we need people to get mad and to stay mad—mad enough that they're willing to spend their energy and treasure on the raging culture wars. When the cockeyed optimist assures his fellow men that all is well, that indeed a sleeping giant of dedicated retrogrades will invariably arise to win the culture wars, despite losing battles with alarming frequency, he squelches their righteous anger. After all, if all is well, then there is no need for mobilization going forward. Blind optimism disincentivizes necessary and fruitful engagement by retrogrades because it prematurely claims victory solely on the basis that people notice and object to the acts of radicals. Thus, the rank sentimentalist who suggests that goodness is somehow destined to prevail in the temporal struggle should be the object of the retrograde's scorn. Such a man has yet to wrap his mind around theodicy and the "mystery of iniquity."

The sleeping giant metaphor lulls would-be agitators into an undue passivity, since it wrongly assumes that wheels are in motion that will culminate in the undoing of radicals' misdeeds. It essentially conflates people's initial reflexive outrage over perceived injustices with organized and efficacious political engagement. It assumes that because people are angry, they will direct their anger into the proper channels by which change may be effected. This is akin to confusing potential energy with kinetic energy. The fact that a political or cultural injustice wrought by radicals irks the consciences of the masses is a mere starting point—it's an aggregation of potential energy. But in order to do any good, this potential energy needs to be *actualized* and released through political organization and transformed into political movement, whether in speech, demonstrations, volunteerism, or capital donation. If initial outrage is never actualized into political movement, then it evaporates with the oscillations of the human mind, or slowly dies out, like a fire having burnt through all its fuel. So, the rousing of people's passions in response to an injustice should not be received as a victory in and of itself. Rather, it should be viewed as a starting point by which, through methodically directed political engagement, true victory can one day be achieved.

And since the sleeping giant metaphor undercuts efficacious political engagement, snuffing it out while it's
still in inchoate form, the metaphor is to be removed
from the retrograde's vocabulary.

Rule 34

Never deny being a retrograde: looking feckless, you'll be called one anyway.

Peter denied Christ thrice and fooled no one, looking only a coward, fumbling and playing for time. Denying or watering down one's retrograde principles results in the *worst* of both worlds: the denier or mitigator forfeits both his honesty and his principle.

Dishonest cowards are the denizens of "no man's land." One unwilling to go to bat for his friend—or to be included as a fellow traveler—*deserves* no friends. There's nothing less honorable than selling out your own title and your own people. For all their want of principle, radicals understand this one well.

Denying membership among the retrogrades comprises the ultimate form of "bad optics" for conservatives.

It happens far too frequently in politics and culture. Remember the fair-weather friend back in the middle school cafeteria who shared your values but who always had one eye on membership in another social group? Long wistful of sexier social standing, this fair-weather friend proves the worst sort of opportunist, one who abandons his camp in the face of the first tormentor or detractor. That middle school friendship was doomed to die an early death all along. But that ignobility is reserved for middle school, right? Adult culture and politics have been ennobled by age and experience, right? No way.

Conversely, true friends are stalwarts. As such, they are as rare in "grown-up" America as in middle school. Retrogrades are dear friends and brethren—fellows you haven't met yet. Unlike most of the other *Rules for Retrogrades*, the majority of retrogrades already know and cherish this one by instinct. Own who you are; boldly be one of your own people; defend your brothers at arms by proudly donning the shield and crest.

All this involves a most critical distinction: in the implementation of these rules, act wholly without hesitation or apology, *but avoid needless heat.* Many retrogrades will be befuddled by this subtle yet vital distinction, because when wrongly understood, it sounds very much like something a moderate would say. Yet in reality, it proves to be nothing of the sort. While never denying who he is, the retrograde must choose his battles wisely. For once engaged in battle, the retrograde can never back down: the single battle that cannot be afforded is the middle school treachery of opportunistic turncoats. Become who you were born to be: a retrograde!

Rule 35

Retrogrades will never be able to profitably wield divisive group politics.

As the One Ring of Power from Tolkien's Middle Earth answers only to Sauron, divisive group politics—the system of political grievance-mongering and favoritism based on race/sex/protected-class—can only deftly be wielded by wicked men, by radicals. Splintering and factionalizing men, turning brother against brother, is hateful connivance. Branding people indelibly with a pre-fabricated identity and de-individualizing them due to a singular attribute is an affront to human dignity, it's an affront to free will. Good men cannot, without losing their souls in the process, embrace such a disordered method. There's no such thing as a man that's wicked in only one respect, since gravely disordered conduct in a particular instance is a mere symptom of a more fundamental problem with the will. "For whoever keeps the whole law and yet stumbles at just one point is guilty of breaking all of it" (Jas 2:10). So, by definition, the retrograde has no recourse to divisive group politics. The minute he attempts to wield them, he ceases to be a retrograde, just like men who die wearing one of the rings forged by Sauron cease to be men and become wraiths.

Application bears out the foolishness of any retrograde dalliances with divisive group politics. First of all, impelled as retrogrades are to refrain from doing evil so that good may come of it, they will always be at a comparative disadvantage with wicked men who are willing to employ unscrupulous political stratagems in furtherance of crooked ends. So, even in the event that the retrograde takes leave of his senses to the point where he contemplates exploring the gloomy method of race/sex/protected-class pandering, he will not be able to wield such politics to the fullest extent, his hand being stayed by his lingering sense of compunction.

In other words, we will never be able to out-radical radicals; we'll never be able to pay a higher ransom for votes than they. Radicals are not hamstrung by ethics in their methods the way retrogrades are. For radicals, the ends justify the means. Putting aside for now the tension of the following hypotheticals with constitutionalism, subsidiarity, and justice, let's suppose that the retrograde were, in an effort at ingratiation, to offer to black Americans reparations for the horrors of slavery; radicals, being unmoored from moral concerns, would simply offer greater reparations. Supposing retrogrades offered a generous package of welfare benefits to illegal immigrants, radicals would simply offer more welfare benefits. Supposing retrogrades offered guaranteed paid maternity leave for working mothers, radicals would simply offer more paid leave. And if retrogrades should attempt to keep pace with radicals in their purchasing of allegiance, then we will have become, for all intents and purposes, indistinguishable from the very ideologues that we claim to oppose. We cannot afford to try to beat radicals at their own cynical game. To do so would mean forfeiting our souls and conceding the very principles that make our movement great.

Neither may we have recourse to the twin swords of despair and envy, which play an integral role in advancing divisive group politics. The diabolical logic behind radicals' adherence to the politics of despair and envy is rather plain. We clearly live in a pluralistic society, one composed of numerous race/sex/protected-class groups with varying interests. So, if radicals can convince a sufficient number of such groups that their interests are in conflict and competition with the interests of one collective bogeyman (i.e., the much maligned "straight, white male"), then radicals can create an artificial cohesion between the various race/sex/protected-class groups by mobilizing them against the bogeyman group. It's the old adage "the enemy of my enemy is my friend."

If radicals can convince the race/sex/protected-class groups that they're dedicated to serving the groups' interests, then the groups will have been consolidated into a dependable radical voting bloc. If the membership in the groups eventually eclipses the membership in the bogeyman group, then radicals will forever hold the reins of power. This is why radicals want to flood the country with illegal aliens; it's why they're encouraging more people to come out of the closet as "gay"; it's why they're constantly telling blacks the lie that racism is still widespread; it's why they're against assimilation and aspirations for a trans-racial national identity; it's why they're constantly telling women that retrogrades want to strip them of civil rights. They need to grow their coalition so that, in the aggregate, it becomes more numerous than the retrograde bloc. This is how radicals grow and mollify their base: at the expense of the unity and confraternity of the nation. In their lust for power, radicals need to divide the country so that they can vanquish the old order, represented in caricature by the straight, white male.

But retrogrades may not do this in reverse—we have too much honor. We are prohibited, in conscience, from drawing on the schadenfreude and resentment that the "have-nots" harbor for the "haves." We are prohibited from stoking provincial inter-race and inter-sex rivalries in an attempt to benefit our political cause; we're prohibited from floating ourselves on the chests of drowning men. The retrograde may not incite his brothers against one another, attempting to build unity through division. We may not rob Peter to pay Paul in order to win hearts and minds. A faction bound together only by the hatred of a common enemy is dysfunctional to the core.

While the pessimistic strategy of incitement *does* work to produce cheap political wins (it's why radicals use this method), the morally-upright retrograde method is a juggernaut in its own right. Our strength lies in the fact that our worldview is the correct one, and in the fact that truth is on our side. The human intellect was made by God so that men could come to know truth. The intellect, therefore, has a natural affinity for the truth. For mankind, truth is intrinsically attractive, attractive *per se*. Those opposed to truth have to use cheap gimmicks and deception of every stripe to attract followers. But not retrogrades. All we need is a platform from which to speak and ready ears and open hearts in our listeners. If retrogrades speak the truth boldly, never being cowed into silence, never allowing radicals to dictate what we can and can't say, we will win the culture and retain our honor in the process. In the end, tawdry gimmicks are no match for gritty substance.

Rule 36

Young retrogrades should be neither sheep nor wolves, but sheepdogs.

Young men should be taught to fight according to the mantra, "never start fights, but finish them." Being smart or proficient at debate is no longer good enough in 2019 America. The time for flabby, comfortable, conservative leisure is at an end. The battle of ideas is quickening to the point at which it will soon become an actual battle. Hence our last few rules involve grouping and preparatory criteria: *who* and *how* to prepare.

We are mustering to stand and fight not only retrogrades but all men of good will who may be counted upon. But first, retrogrades must make *themselves* worthy of a fight. Rocky did not fight Apollo without a rigorous training regimen executed over a grueling period of time. Radicals categorically avoid non-rigged exchanges of ideas—where they cannot interrupt or yell—because they are aware that they are fated to fail in contests of ideas. It was the radical Marx who said that the purpose of philosophy is not understanding the world but changing it. The radicals do not care if their formulations are correct. They only care about power. This explains why they turn to displays of semi-force and outright force instead of learning from their errors in debate. Only good men heed their past errors. Radicals simply learn how to implement force, giving the flimsy appearance of righteousness to wrong conclusions.

A retrograde must be able to stand down any radical, when the eventuality of the radical's defeat in the battle of wits inevitably coaxes forth the violent response from him. While such a statement did not correctly modify the status of the world a decade or two ago, it is one of the final and most important rules for retrogrades: *prepare for battle.* Hopefully, the battle won't be necessary. But this hope for peace grows more foolish as each day passes.

To this end, the retrograde must maintain physical fitness in order to maintain—rather, to regain—the imposing male standard of the West. While not every man has the time or training or talent to become proficient in the martial arts, virtually every man has thirty minutes per day to train at home with weights. That way, even a martially untrained retrograde can exercise an imposing presence in the public defense of ideas.

Rule 37

You don't need to be a member of a certain class of people to address an issue related to or stemming from said class of people.

I often hear radicals brushing off retrograde arguments solely on the basis that the retrograde making a point is not a member of the class that would be affected by his policy proposal. One often hears, when debating affirmative action, things like, "What would a white man know about struggles to overcome discrimination?" When debating abortion, one often hears tropes like, "What interest does a man have in a discussion of women's bodies?" When speaking of redefining marriage to accommodate the perverted lusts of homosexuals, we hear, "What interest does a privileged, straight, cis-gendered man have in controlling whom people may 'love'?"

The asinine presumption underlying these pointed questions is that one can only know truth from experience, as opposed to reasoning to it *a priori*. No one, not even the most obtuse radicals, actually believes this though. If it were the case that only someone in a class directly affected by a law should be able to lend his voice to a public policy debate thereon, then only suicide victims could lobby for or against anti-suicide laws. If it were the case, then only people who had previously jumped off a cliff could warn their friends not to jump off a cliff. The nature of the human intellect is such that we don't need to have experienced the effects of an idea as precondition for saying that the idea is good or bad. We have the power of deduction, the power of reasoning that guides us to determine whether something is good or evil before we've experienced it firsthand. If we could only know things experientially, then Adam and Eve would have been justified in eating the forbidden fruit, because prior to eating it, they wouldn't have been able to know whether it was truly good for them or bad for them.

Radicals try to control who can say things in an effort to silence the maximum amount of dissenting voices. It redounds to the benefit of radicals to set the ground rules of debate in a way that precludes as many erudite retrograde voices as possible from entering into a policy discussion. Do not ever let a radical tell you that you are the wrong "type" of person to make a point. To put one's finger on the scale of public discourse is to control it's outcome. We cannot abide this.

The idea that only members of a certain class can opine about matters particularly affecting that class has been silently incorporated even into conservative praxis. Right-wing news outlets, when staging a discussion of a sensitive issue that is widely seen as being particularly intertwined with a specific group's interests, will predictably trot out a panel composed exclusively of members of the group, so as to avoid the danger of being called "racist," "sexist," or any other "-ist" that comprises radicals' arsenal of groundless slanders, for daring to allow an unartificially-constrained group of humans to enter into productive dialogue. When a debate over affirmative action takes place on the news, we can count on all panelists being black. When a debate over government-subsidized contraception takes place, we can count on all panelists being women. When a debate over illegal immigration takes place, the media thinks it's a nifty trick to have all participants be of Mexican heritage.

This well-accepted practice is actually a serious injustice. When a person is wronged, he should be the one to advocate on behalf of and vindicate his interests. The fact is, the argument against affirmative action is that it *discriminates* against whites and Asians in favor of blacks. Hence, any debate panel on affirmative action should take pains to incorporate a white or Asian participant, affording members of the offended class a chance to vindicate their own interests. Any debate panel on feminism should take pains to incorporate men, because it is men's rights and prerogatives that have been appropriated by women in the wake of the feminist movement. (In fact, one often hears, even in conservative circles, that it's up to women to rise up and repudiate feminism. No. No. No. Women have done enough. *Men* need to rise up and repudiate feminism, taking back what's rightfully ours. The answer for disorder isn't more disorder.) It is precisely because one does a more thorough job at advancing his own interests instead of those of others that the American legal system is adversarial in nature.

Never fall into the trap of allowing radicals to dictate who is the "right" type of person to address an issue. They invariably come to the wrong conclusion, a conclusion whose sole purpose is to handicap the retrograde movement by silencing as many of our voices as they can. If you are the party aggrieved by a radical policy, do not allow radicals to excise you from the public debate on the issue because you are the wrong color or sex. Insist on vindicating your rights personally or through a representative of your interest group. Do this and we will forever maim radicals' ability to wield divisive group politics. Do this and we will have a chance to make our voices heard clearly going forward.

Rule 38

Under no circumstances let radicals control the rules of the game.

If an active participant in a game were able to set the game's rules in real time, and if he were at the same time an unscrupulous man, in his zeal to win, he'd certainly concoct rules favorable to himself, all but ensuring his victory. Unilateral power to set rules imbues the rule maker with godlike invincibility. Scenarios such as these are thinly-veiled "Calvinball"— the game from *Calvin and Hobbes* where the main character, Calvin, initiates an endless series of rule changes, all designed to set himself up to win.

In war, you don't let your enemy dictate the terms of the battle to you. If you want to give yourself the best chance of achieving victory, you fight on your own terms. If possible, you don't fight in the enemy's chosen setting; you fight on your own terrain. You don't fight with weapons favored by the enemy; you fight with the weapons he fears the most. You don't fight him at a time when he expects it; you fight him at the time he least expects it. You don't fight with tactics the enemy prefers; you fight him with tactics of which he's ignorant.

Radicals have long been dictating to conservatives our rules of engagement, the rules controlling the outcome of our battle. Radicals have made a habit out of dictating those topics which are acceptable in public discourse. Through the bludgeon of political correctness, they've assumed the power to tell us what language we can use (and what language we can't use) when describing a problem. We can no longer speak our minds with clear diction. Instead, we're told to use muddled niceties out of sensitivity to the feelings of an ostensible victim class. Yet radicals can spew vitriol at retrogrades with impunity.

Under the present Calvinball regime, for radicals, dissent against an unfavored administration is "patriotic." On the other hand, when retrogrades dissent against an administration favored by radicals, it's "an affront to the dignity of the office." Radicals can stage sit-ins and "occupy" vast areas of critical urban centers for weeks at a time to protest income inequality, but retrogrades must have a "buffer zone" to pray in front of abortion clinics. Radicals are free to hold gay-pride parades in any locale in the nation, but retrogrades have to fight tooth and nail to get a permit for a straight-pride parade in one city. Bigotry against Christians and Jews is openly embraced by radicals; yet, if a retrograde so much as hints that Islam may be prone to violence, they are branded as hateful and "Islamophobic." In fact, anytime a retrograde reproaches some evil that radicals favor, we're called "phobic" for doing so (e.g., "homophobic,"

"Islamophobic," "fatphobic," "transphobic," and "xeno-phobic"). Retrogrades have allowed ourselves to be hapless victims of bullying for too long, acting like the overly passive friend who knows his peer is cheating at a board game but does nothing about it. This paradigm must be altered, and it must be altered fast.

If retrogrades are to prevail in the ongoing political-cultural war, we cannot resign ourselves to sheepishness in the face of radical imperiousness. There's nothing to stop us from insisting on our own set of rules. And when radicals are forced to play on our turf, let's see who prevails.

Rule 39

The retrograde rejects any and all racist, statist, anti-Christian, anti-Semitic perversions of conservatism associated with the "alt-right." Alt-right is non-right: it is false conservatism— ideological refuse to be identified, decried, and jettisoned.

Intellectually, the alt-right worldview proves to be piffle, folderol, without pedigree. But practically, as a stalking horse in the popular mind for Catholic conservatism, it presents the mortal danger of mistaken identity.

The radical news and commentary media will hasten to identify retrogrades as "alt-right" because they customarily slander all non-moderate, non-tepid opposition parties in this boilerplate fashion. It is the new standard of radical Western journalism: depict any and all parties rejecting one-world-government and instead espousing national sovereignty as "alt-right."

Simply put, to be retrograde is to pose a superlative threat to the radical-mainstream: we are the one true movement of classical anti-racism and anti-bigotry. Radicals will never be deterred from their calumnious false narrative by hard facts, however. The retrograde worldview insists on patriotism, borders, and "turning back the clock" for a highly specific reason: love of Christ and his moral code. The alt-right worldview merely apes these sympathies from a tawdry resentment for the Christian teleology which insinuates them.

These alt-right rogues can easily be popularly confused for retrogrades because they customarily "fight nuclear" like retrogrades. Like that of the retrogrades, alt-right rhetoric lacks the doddering, domestic impotence of the mod-cons. The alt-right is possessed of some fire in the belly, which makes it stand out amongst moderate mainstream wordplay. But their wicked principles are basically, diametrically opposed to ours.

The real secret behind the radical rush to characterize alt-right as conservatism inheres in the fact that alt-right is actually nothing more than the anti-globalist alt-left! Both rivals of the retrograde—radicals and alt-right—prove to be materialistic egalitarians who favor "mob rule" democratic institutions which reject the timelessness of the immutable natural law and the dignity of the individual. Consider the identical nature of the radical left and the alt-right on the following substantial issues: they both favor centrally planned, socialist economy; they both fixate on a determinist view of race and personal identity (whereas the retrograde adopts a position of Thomistic, colorblind individualism); they both harbor a cultural and policy antipathy to Christianity and a longing for a "robust and binding" surrogate for it; each side cherishes abortion, population control, and eugenics.

Moreover, modern radicalism is often implicitly neo-pagan whereas the alt-right is explicitly neo-pagan. Consider this passage from an article in *Vice*:

> There's a war going on in the American Pagan community. On one side are racists who see gods like Odin and Thor as an embodiment of the supremacy whites have over the rest of the planet. On the other are the practitioners who believe these gods transcend racial lines and belong to everyone. Recently, the contention between these two groups has reached a tipping point as anti-racist pagans try to claim the narrative around their faith before it is overtaken by alt-right racists. Although the leaders of Nazi Germany were obsessed with Paganism and the occult, it has largely been associated with multiculturalism here in the United States.[33]

Like all paganism, all bigotry, all eugenics, all anti-Christianity, all collectivism: alt-right is to be repudiated wherever the retrograde encounters it (which is practically nowhere except on the internet, given the alt-right's exaggerated yet small presence in American life).

---

[33]   https://www.vice.com/en_us/article/59kq93/racists-are-threatening-to-take-over-paganism.

Rule 40

Victory loves preparation.

This is perhaps both the most fundamental of the *Rules for Retrogrades*, and the most crucial. It is nothing short of pure hubris to think that we stand any chance of winning a fight against a competent opponent for which we are not adequately prepared. Leading up to a bout, boxers spend months in training camps immersed in fitness routines, sparring with fighters chosen based on their physical and technical similarity to the upcoming opponent; before a match, chessmasters spend weeks poring over the opening choices, stylistic preferences, and prior games of their rivals; generals meticulously study the tactics and methods of opposing generals (General Patton, in the run-up to the North Africa campaign in World War Two, famously read Erwin Rommel's book, *Infantry Attacks*); football coaches sit down weekly to watch film of their upcoming opponents, to get familiar with their roster strengths and playbooks. Why mod-cons believe for a second that they have a snowflake's chance in hell of whupping an organized, bankrolled, determined group of radicals just by showing up at the polls every two years and perhaps bloviating to insolent nieces and nephews about politics over Thanksgiving dinner is one of the unsolved mysteries of the universe.

Too many mod-cons earnestly think that, because they're nominally on the side of the good, providence has all but guaranteed them victory in the political-cultural wars. Too many mod-cons believe that their only duty to their fellow men is to "be productive members of society," hold down a steady job, produce a milquetoast family without getting a divorce, harm no one, perhaps go to church on Sunday, and develop acceptably partisan political opinions. They've got another think coming. While "victory rests with the Lord," the horse is to be "made ready for the day of battle." Living an uninspired, ennui-filled, suburban existence replete with creature comforts of every sort doesn't lend itself to wresting control of the West away from radicals hell-bent on destroying it. As Marvelous Marvin Hagler famously quipped, "It's tough to get out of bed to do roadwork at 5 a.m. when you've been sleeping in silk pajamas." Taking a generally passive approach to the pressing issues of our day, albeit with the tired rationalization that one "wants to help but doesn't have time to get involved" is really just sterilized treason against the retrograde cause. What we need is active and uncompromising engagement. And this takes preparation.

How can retrogrades prepare themselves to fight and win the political-cultural wars? First, we must take great pains to prepare ourselves intellectually for ideological combat. The retrograde must be well-versed in classical works of Western political thought, in the philosophy of natural rights and limited government, in the justifications for the free market, in the social kingship of Jesus Christ, and in the doctrines of Christianity. In order to do battle, one must know with great specificity the objectives of the fight—especially when the battle is to take place in the realm of ideas. Achieving a foundational knowledge of the retrograde philosophy is condition precedent for jumping into the fray. Without it, our engagement would be directionless and flailing, and we'd suffer significant attrition to radicals. And no, watching Tucker Carlson every night isn't sufficient either (although God bless him).

Once the retrograde has a foundational understanding of his own worldview, then he must think about taking a more active role in seizing the culture. Seasoning his knowledge with prudence, the retrograde should identify what he believes to be the most pressing issues of the day (and it's okay and even salutary to have some variation here). He then needs to band together with other retrogrades interested in advocating those priority issues and form a group (or join one, if a suitable one already exists). The retrograde must make a firm and realistic pledge of his time to the group, going forward; it is insufficient to conditionally give time when it can be worked into the margins of one's schedule. The present state of cultural decay does not admit of dilettantism. Once the retrograde has involved himself with like-minded men, he and his compatriots must come up with a proposal for making headway on the identified issue, for ushering in the retrograde vision. Once a proposal is agreed upon, it should be formalized and written into an agenda, with specific dates and times assigned for specific actions. The retrograde compatriots must continue to meet and should make every attempt to bring additional friends and acquaintances to their meetings so as to swell our numbers. For every retrograde issue, there must be permanent retrograde organization. This is the only efficacious sort of political involvement. Showing up at the polls and making idle chatter about politics is *assumed*—it's necessary but not sufficient.

The retrograde must also become a student of radicalism. Not only must he be well-versed in his own literature, the retrograde must be just as well-versed in *radicals'* literature. He must know precisely what it is that the radical believes and why the radical believes it. One is badly and unnecessarily handicapped in trying to fight an enemy that he doesn't quite understand. If retrogrades settle for a superficial knowledge of radicals' goals, we will never understand why it is that radicals do what they do, as they're doing it. We'll never understand the method, the uniting cause, underlying what might appear to the untrained eye as random and unconnected planks in their platform. One can only fight an enemy effectively when he understands the enemy's overarching goals. It's why America's policy of "containment" really did prove effective in bringing down communism. Our generals knew that, of its very nature, communism could not survive if it were not a worldwide system; it could not perdure if relegated to nation-states alone. Hence, by curtailing its spread, we were able to have it wither from inside out. We must apply the same general principle in defeating radicalism: understand its meta-strategy and its *sine qua nons* and sketch out a way to sabotage it, like the Star Wars Rebel Alliance analyzing the death star plans to find and exploit a weakness.

The foregoing are all mere examples of preparatory steps that retrogrades must take in advance of their entry into the political-cultural wars. If we are to prevail, we must out-prepare and out-work our ideological enemy. We must eschew the complacency and passivity of mod-cons, which was at its zenith when the Boomers lost the culture for us in the first place, fifty years ago. If we inculcate discipline and commit ourselves to the tough path ahead, we give ourselves the chance to remake the West into a shining beacon on a hill.

Epilogue

"My brothers, I see in your eyes the same fear that would take the heart of me. A day may come when the courage of men fails, when we forsake our friends and break all bonds of fellowship. But it is not this day. An hour of wolves and shattered shields when the Age of Men comes crashing down. But it is not this day! This day we fight! By all that you hold dear on this good Earth, I bid you stand, Men of the West!"

—Aragorn, Son of Arathorn, Battle of Morannon